WARRIORS
OF THE WORD

THE BIBLE MEMORIZATION BATTLE GUIDE
FOR WINNING SPIRITUAL VICTORIES

AARON & EMILY HOUSE

PIERCING
WORD

Warriors of the Word

The Bible Memorization Battle Guide for Winning Spiritual Victories

Special Edition

by Aaron and Emily House

© 2021 by Piercing Word, Inc.

Published by
Piercing Word, Inc.
1821 Oregon Pike, Suite 210,
Lancaster, PA 17601
www.piercingword.org

Published 2021.
Printed in the United States of America.

ISBN 978-0-578-88904-7

This book is dedicated to God
and to our fellow brothers and sisters in Christ
who want to know and love God more by memorizing His Word.

CONTENTS

Boot Camp Packing List

Before you join us at our Bible Memorization Boot Camp, there are few helpful things we'd like to "throw in your bag" so you are prepared during the training process.

The Piercing Word Bible Memorization Process is what we have been teaching for years in our Bible Memorization Workshops around the globe. It is simple and yet profound. The chapters in this book follow this structure. As you finish each chapter, you will see which step in the process we have completed.

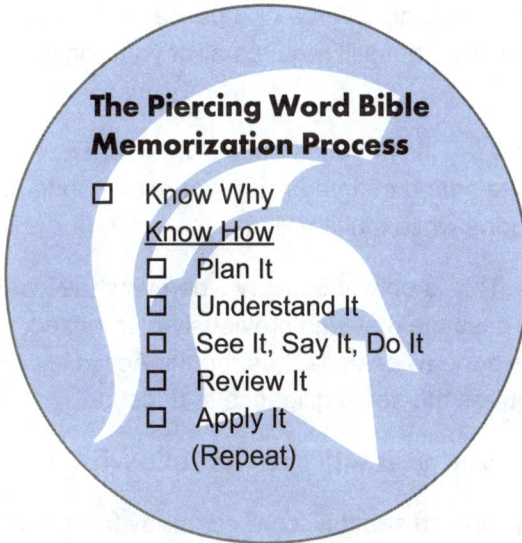

The Piercing Word Bible Memorization Process

☐ Know Why

Know How
- ☐ Plan It
- ☐ Understand It
- ☐ See It, Say It, Do It
- ☐ Review It
- ☐ Apply It

(Repeat)

The only step that does not have its own chapter is "Repeat." This does *not* mean to repeat the Bible passage you are memorizing, although you will be learning how to do that in creative and effective ways in this book. Repeat means to repeat the process. Why? Because we desire for Bible memorization to become a lifelong spiritual discipline for every believer in Jesus Christ. Our hope is that, no matter where you are in your spiritual walk, you will take up the sword of the Spirit and continue your training in the Word of God.

Memorization Definitions

Pre-memorization—This is time spent reading, listening to, or studying the text with the purpose of truly understanding it. The goal of this time is to understand, not to memorize. However, the understanding gained in this phase is essential before moving into the Active Memorization phase.

Active Memorization—This is a one-time memorization experience with a specific and attainable goal and set time frame. You are alone, with limited distractions, using 100 percent of your focus and attention on memorization.

Solidification Review—This happens every day for at least a week after actively memorizing a verse or a passage. It can be done by yourself or with a friend, but still requires all of your focus and attention.

Maintenance Review—This happens once a week or once a month for an indefinite period of time or until you move on to another passage. It can be done while multitasking.

Re-memorization—This is only necessary when you have waited too long to review a passage that was previously memorized. Although this can be done twice as fast as regular Active Memorization, it requires the same diligence and focus.

Throughout this book, you will see the following icons:

VICTORY STORY When you see this icon, get ready for a real-life story. We have sprinkled these throughout the book to encourage you in your own journey. Each Victory Story is an authentic boots-on-the-ground battle account from a spiritual warrior who has wielded their Scripture memory weapon against the forces of evil in the heavenly places (see Ephesians 6:12).

SWORDPLAY TIP Throughout the book we have scattered fun and insightful tips to aid you in your memorization journey. Utilize these highlighted truths to enhance your skill of wielding the sword of God's Word in the spiritual battles of your own life.

At the end of each chapter, there are some tangible action steps for you to take. These exercises will be integral to your training as you seek to become a Warrior of the Word. Be sure to complete these drills as you finish each chapter.

Every time you see one of these name graphics, you will know whether Aaron or Emily is writing that section. The author voice will remain the same even through headings and subheadings until you see the next name graphic.

At the back of this book, you will find:
The Arsenal
The Arsenal is kind of like an appendix, only cooler. It's a collection of Bible passages that have been specifically outfitted for your warrior training. This is a place you can go to select your spiritual weapons. You might just find one there that fits you perfectly.

Battle Resources
The Battle Resources section includes workbook-style sheets for you to fill out as a part of your warrior training as well as additional resources to take you deeper in your memorization skills. This will be a place you return to at the end of each chapter as you use it to build your own Bible memorization plan— what we like to call your Plan of Attack.

Online Resources

Warriorsofthewordbook.org
Visit our website for downloadable content including a free printable Workbook as well as a Personal Memorization Plan Calculator Tool.

Warriors of the Word Facebook Group
Join the community of Bible Memorizers to find encouragement, camaraderie, and accountability. Scan this QR code to enter this private group where you can confidently share your struggles, your victory stories, as well as pictures and videos of your journey. You can also access this group through our website – warriorsofthewordbook.org.

A Tale of Two Warriors

Our Story

When the righteous cry for help, the Lord hears
 and delivers them out of all their troubles.
The Lord is near to the brokenhearted
 and saves the crushed in spirit.
Many are the afflictions of the righteous,
 but the Lord delivers him out of them all. . . .
The Lord redeems the life of his servants;
 none of those who take refuge in him will be condemned.
~ Psalm 34:17–19, 22

I smiled gently at my wife as she gazed at me from her pillow and swiped salty tears away from her eyes. I said, "If I am going to read this to you every day, I guess I might as well just memorize it." I had just finished reading Psalm 34 to her for what seemed like the hundredth time that week. Emily had recently suffered a second early-term miscarriage and was grieving heavily. Falling asleep at night was particularly difficult for her. As the distractions of the day slowed and darkness enveloped the atmosphere, her questions and sorrow would pour forth. Anytime she was tempted to question the goodness of God during this time or felt drawn toward hopelessness, she would ask me to read Psalm 34 and remind her of the truth.

AARON

So I committed Psalm 34 to memory, and my wife continued to request that I read that passage. But now, instead of reading, I could quote it to her anytime, anywhere.

> I will bless the Lord at all times;
> > his praise shall continually be in my mouth.
> My soul makes its boast in the Lord;
> > let the humble hear and be glad.
> Oh, magnify the Lord with me,
> > and let us exalt his name together!
> I sought the Lord, and he answered me
> > and delivered me from all my fears.
> Those who look to him are radiant,
> > and their faces shall never be ashamed. (Psalm 34:1–5)

I found myself comforting her with the words of Psalm 34 as we drove down the highway, as we took a walk in the neighborhood, or as she grappled with hearing yet another friend's pregnancy announcement. As we both clung to the goodness of God proclaimed by the truths in this passage, we grew closer to God and to each other.

Emily memorized Psalm 34 as well and continued to let the intense grief drive her to more and more Scripture, drinking in God's promises of hope. She clung to passages such as Romans 4, praying for faith like Abraham: "In hope he believed against hope. . . . He did not weaken in faith when he considered his own body, which was as good as dead. . . . No unbelief made him waver concerning the promise of God, but grew strong in his faith as he gave glory to God, fully convinced that God was able to do what he had promised" (Romans 4:18–21).

As Emily soaked her mind in God's truth, I saw her begin to transform from the inside out. She chose hope when she felt hopeless. She sang praises to God in her grief and felt peace rush over her as she fixed her eyes on our unchanging, glorious Creator and Father. She became a firmer believer that God is good all the time than she was before experiencing such poignant personal loss. Only the Holy Spirit can cultivate such dynamic change in a soul. I watched Emily continue to cling to God's Word as she cradled our firstborn son in her womb, preaching Psalm 34 aloud to her anxious heart. Now, years later, God has redeemed every tear in the beautiful faces of our three healthy children. And these days, if you could sneak a peek into the moonlit nursery, you just might hear Emily or me whispering the truths of Psalm 34 to the little bundle nestled in our arms. "I will bless the Lord at all times . . . ."

This is what memorizing Scripture is all about. You may at first think that memorizing the majority of the New Testament and reciting Revelation before a public audience

> **SWORDPLAY TIP**
>
> **The spiritual discipline you employ now will prepare you to wield the sword of God's Word and experience dynamic victories in the days to come.**

was the climax of my Bible memorization journey, but it wasn't. If anything, the climax of my Bible memorization journey has come in the dirty realities of life when my boots hit the ground. Walking through our miscarriage grief journey with my wife was not fun. But it was during that time that knowing God's Word by heart became more than a spiritual discipline. It became a necessity. Now we were prepared with the spiritual tools to press into God's truth when we needed it the most. Chances are your journey will take a similar turn. The spiritual discipline you employ now will prepare you to wield the sword of God's Word and experience victories in the days to come.

Our lives are riddled with spiritual battles that many of us have never properly prepared for. Scripture says,

> Be strong in the Lord and in the strength of his might. Put on the whole armor of God, that you may be able to stand against the schemes of the devil. For we do not wrestle against flesh and blood, but against the rulers, against the authorities, against the cosmic powers over this present darkness, against the spiritual forces of evil in the heavenly places. Therefore take up the whole armor of God, that you may be able to withstand in the evil day, and having done all, to stand firm. Stand therefore, having fastened on the belt of truth, and having put on the breastplate of righteousness, and, as shoes for your feet, having put on the readiness given by the gospel of peace. In all circumstances take up the shield of faith, with which you can extinguish

EMILY

all the flaming darts of the evil one; and take the helmet of salvation, and the sword of the Spirit, which is the word of God, praying at all times in the Spirit, with all prayer and supplication. (Ephesians 6:10–18)

Our battle is not against flesh and blood; it is a spiritual battle. Our enemies are not the people around us. Rather, they are the spiritual forces at work within and around those people. Satan is constantly attacking us with temptations of fear, doubt, lust, pride, hate, jealousy, and countless other sins. It doesn't matter how strong, smart, beautiful, or rich we are—those physical earthly attributes will do nothing against spiritual powers. Therefore, we must fight with spiritual weapons.

Take a closer look at the passage. What is the only offensive weapon that is listed? The sword of the Spirit, which is the word of God. What we wage war with is what proceeds from the mouth of God, together with prayer. Every other weapon listed is a defensive weapon. And where do we get the rest of the armor? We must fasten on the belt of truth. How do we learn what truth is? God's Word. We are called to put on the breastplate of righteousness, which is only possible by believing in the Jesus of the Bible. What about the gospel of peace? This is the gospel, or good news, that the whole Bible proclaims. How about the helmet of salvation? Salvation is found in the good news of Jesus, which is found in the treasure of his Word. And lastly, the shield of faith. Scripture says, "Faith comes from hearing, and hearing through the word of Christ" (Romans 10:17).

Engaging with Scripture will help empower us to don each piece of spiritual armor. One of the most influential ways we can engage with the Word of God is by memorizing it. As we rehearse and meditate on the Scripture in our mind and let it soak into our spirit, we can begin to say with the psalmist,

> I have hidden your word in my heart
> that I might not sin against you. (Psalm 119:11 NIV)

Don't miss the integral role of the Holy Spirit in the armor of God. The Bible is even called "the sword of the Spirit," and we are to always be "praying in the Spirit." So God's Word is vital, and the Holy Spirit is just as essential. Some Christians are almost tempted to ignore the Holy Spirit entirely and make the Trinity into God the Father, God the Son, and God the Holy Bible. This may sound ridiculous, but this is how many Christians live. This is not the triune God we serve. We serve God the Father, God the Son, and God the Holy Spirit—three in one. The Holy Spirit is the person of the Trinity who has been given to us to work supernaturally in our lives, and he cannot be ignored. At the same time, there are other Christians who rely so entirely on the Holy Spirit that they neglect the Bible, and they end up straying from the truth. The Holy Bible is the main vehicle God has used to convey his story and his heart for us, and it cannot be neglected. We must have a constant filling of both the Spirit and the Word if we desire to live godly lives in this present age.

If we said to you, "Jesus changes lives," you would probably respond with a resounding "Amen!" But let me tell you something profound. Memorizing Scripture has changed how both of us walk with Jesus. In this book you will continue to see how and why this life-giving spiritual discipline has changed our lives. Our hope and prayer is that our story and the stories of those people contained within this book will spark a wildfire of desire in your soul for God's Word. May the Holy Spirit set the church aflame, so that the world will watch us burn with passion for our Savior!

Memorizing Scripture has helped release me from the plague of lust and rage. It has made me more like Christ in holiness and righteousness. Memorizing God's Word has given me the confidence and ability to speak hard truth to a brother in Christ when he needs to hear it most. It has given me the words to speak when sharing my faith with those who haven't yet come to faith in Christ. Memorizing God's Word has grown and bolstered my affections for our Lord and Savior, fascinated me with his ways and truths, brought me into intimate moments of communion with him, given me wisdom in big decisions, educated my relational conflicts,

> **SWORDPLAY TIP**
>
> **Memorizing Scripture will change how you walk with Jesus.**

stirred me out of laziness, and kept me from joining the sins of others through complaining, grumbling, or gossip. It has refined how I walk with Jesus, perhaps more than any other spiritual discipline I have exercised.

As you go through this book, you will be equipped to be able to wield the sword of the Spirit, the Word of God, against Satan and the invisible powers of darkness that plague our world. Spiritual wars are just like physical wars. If you want to win, you don't fight the war alone; you do it with an army. And if you want to win, you use the best weaponry you have access to. In our case, that weapon is God's Word.

We are only two warriors. God is calling you to join together with us and prepare for spiritual battle by knowing him through his Word. Our hope is that this Bible Memorization Battle Guide will equip you for spiritual victories as you become a Warrior of the Word.

CHAPTER 1

Calling for New Recruits
The Need to Memorize Scripture

But as for you, continue in what you have learned and have firmly believed, knowing from whom you learned it and how from childhood you have been acquainted with the sacred writings, which are able to make you wise for salvation through faith in Christ Jesus. All Scripture is breathed out by God and profitable for teaching, for reproof, for correction, and for training in righteousness, that the man of God may be complete, equipped for every good work.
~ 2 Timothy 3:14–16

Running to the Word

"Why is this happening to me? Why can't I just be normal?" I wailed to my mother through tears of pain. "All I want to do is serve God." As I wept, my mother wrapped me tightly in her arms and whispered to me that God had big plans for me. "But who would ever marry *me*?" I retorted. I was so broken. So in need. So different from everyone around me. I was only twelve years old at the time.

I was diagnosed at the age of eight with four different neurological disorders that plagued me throughout my growing-up years and especially during adolescence: Tourette Syndrome, Attention Deficit Hyperactivity Disorder (ADHD), Obsessive Compulsive Disorder

AARON

(OCD), and Rage Disorder. These disorders drove me to physical and vocal tics, hyperactivity, distraction, obsession, and rage on a daily basis. My brother, mother, and father would have to physically restrain me day after day when I went out of control to ensure I did not hurt myself or others or break things in the house. They would physically hold me down until I started to weep and the adrenaline would finally release through my tears. This was a daily ordeal.

Around this same time, I was taking a homeschool Bible class using the Abeka curriculum. I would pop my teacher in the VCR (this was before DVD players and video streaming) and listen to the teachings. This particular Bible teacher challenged us to have a daily quiet time with God. I decided I would take the challenge, and, as my OCD would dictate, I obsessed about it. When I would pop my teacher in the VCR the next morning and realize that I had completely forgotten to spend time with God in his Word, the rage disorder would kick in and I would literally start to hit myself.

By the end of that semester, I was having a daily quiet time in God's Word for about thirty minutes every morning. As I continued in this practice, I began to find peace in God. I was able to rest my fears and my anger at the feet of Jesus. I was convicted of the depth of my sin and realized that even though I had rage disorder that inclined me to anger and rage, my true disorder was a sinful nature. No matter how hard it was to resist the rage when adrenaline was suddenly released into my body, I was still at fault for giving in to the urge. I grew to hate my sin. God began to show me that I was not defined by my sin, but instead, I was and now am separate from my sin through Christ. He revealed deep in my heart that I was not a boy struggling with rage disorder but a child of the living God who had been pulled from the depths of hellish anger and was fighting alongside my Savior to win the daily battles against the enemy, whose purpose was to steal, kill, and destroy.

Those difficult years drove me to God and his Word. God used these disorders to bring me close to him at a young age. In fact, I found such solace in his Word and in my daily times with God that my quiet times grew from thirty minutes a day to a full hour and eventually as a teenager to two solid hours with God every morning. This was a foundational time for me.

While I read God's Word during these precious times in the morning, I realized there were some amazing passages in the Bible that I couldn't just leave on the page. I needed to take them with me. I needed to memorize them, just like I had memorized Bible verses for Bible Drill competitions at our church in years past. As I went along, I started underlining and highlighting verses, chapters, and even whole books that I wanted to memorize. At that point, I began to memorize and internalize God's Word as though my life depended on it; in many ways, it did. It was like water to my thirsty soul. Little did I know that was the moment I began to become a warrior of the Word.

The Value of Bible Memorization

Perhaps you have had a recent experience where you thought, *If only I knew what God had to say about this*. Well, here's the good news; chances are God's heart on that issue is just waiting for you to uncover it in the Bible. Not only that, but you can have that truth with you at all times, even when the world around us is screaming lies into our ears.

Many Christians feel like they understand why we should memorize Scripture and can even spout off a good reason or two for doing Bible memorization. But if we truly understood the value of memorizing God's Word, I think more of us would be practicing this important spiritual discipline.

In this chapter, Emily and I will share with you the most important reasons we have discovered for memorizing God's Word.

Center your identity in Christ

I count everything as loss because of the surpassing worth of knowing Christ Jesus my Lord. For his sake I have suffered the loss of all things and count them as rubbish, in order that I may gain Christ. (Philippians 3:8)

In our American culture, we tend to identify ourselves by our career titles, by our relationships with others, or by what we have accomplished. The apostle Paul did the same thing before he came to know Christ. But after he came into a relationship with Jesus Christ, he resolved "to know nothing . . . except Jesus Christ and him crucified" (1 Corinthians 2:2). In his letter to the church of Philippi, he lists all of his accomplishments and titles. Then he basically says, "Next to Jesus, all my titles and credentials are trash." Wow! Talk about an identity shift. Paul no longer centered his identity in his accomplishments, his titles, his training, his heritage, or his credentials. Paul's new identity was in Christ alone. Memorizing key passages in the Bible can help us center our identity in Christ just as Paul did.

Pray Scripture

> For this reason I bow my knees before the Father, from whom every family in heaven and on earth is named. (Ephesians 3:14–15)

Have you ever wanted to pray for someone but been at a loss of what to say? Praying the words of Scripture over someone is so valuable because you're using God's words, not your own. You already know it is truth and that what you are praying is God's will.

There are many times that I will pray a specific passage over a brother or sister in Christ. For instance, if I am praying for spiritual strength or a deeper knowledge of God, I might pray the words of Paul in Ephesians chapter 3:

> [May you] be strengthened with power through his Spirit in your inner being, so that Christ may dwell in your hearts through faith—that you, being rooted and grounded in love, may have strength to comprehend with all the saints what is the breadth and length and height and depth, and to know the love of Christ that surpasses knowledge, that you may be filled with all the fullness of God. Now to him who is able to do far more abundantly than all that we ask or think, according to the power at work within us, to him be glory in the church and in Christ Jesus throughout all generations, forever and ever. Amen. (Ephesians 3:16–21)

As you can see, I personalized the first couple words and jumped right into the middle of the prayer. If you have a whole biblical prayer memorized, you can start anywhere in the passage and incorporate a portion of it into your own prayers at any time. This kind of Scripture-based prayer has been extremely effective as I am sensitive to what the Lord is doing and how he wants to speak to someone in that moment.

Share your faith

Have no fear of them, nor be troubled, but in your hearts honor Christ the Lord as holy, always being prepared to make a defense to anyone who asks you for a reason for the hope that is in you; yet do it with gentleness and respect, having a good conscience, so that, when you are slandered, those who revile your good behavior in Christ may be put to shame. (1 Peter 3:14–16)

Many of us feel somewhat uncomfortable sharing our faith with others. We feel as though we don't know what to say and that we will somehow mess it up if we try. If we memorize Scriptures that clearly lay out the gospel, it will help us not to be at a loss for words when sharing the good news.

Raymond Yates, one of our past Discipleship Team members, shared with us how the Holy Spirit brought memorized Scripture to his mind during an unexpected opportunity to share his faith: "I was talking to a coworker one day and I was trying to decide how best to share the gospel with him. I just couldn't find the right words to phrase it. And then I remembered that I had actually memorized Ephesians 2. It says that we were dead in our trespasses and sins, in which we once walked, but God had mercy on us and brought us near to him through his Son."

Similarly, if you know God's truth word for word, you will be able to share it clearly, concisely, and with confidence when the Holy Spirit prompts you. Memorizing Scripture in order to be able to share your faith is so important that we consider gospel verses to be some of the most essential verses to memorize. We will discuss this more in the coming chapters.

Encourage others

Let the word of Christ dwell in you richly, teaching and admonishing one another in all wisdom, singing psalms and hymns and spiritual songs, with thankfulness in your hearts to God. (Colossians 3:16)

> Encourage one another and build one another up, just as you are doing. (1 Thessalonians 5:11)

Have you ever attempted to comfort a friend who is going through a hard time and been at a loss for encouraging words? What better way could there possibly be to encourage a friend or family member than with truth straight from the Word of God?

One of the passages I have used most often to encourage others is Philippians 4:5–7. If one of my friends or family members or even a random acquaintance is struggling with anxiety over a certain situation, I have often been able to share the words of God with them in that moment:

> The Lord is at hand; do not be anxious about anything, but in everything by prayer and supplication with thanksgiving let your requests be made known to God. And the peace of God, which surpasses all understanding, will guard your hearts and your minds in Christ Jesus. (Philippians 4:5–7)

Fight temptation and fear with the sword of the Spirit

> For the weapons of our warfare are not of the flesh but have divine power to destroy strongholds. (2 Corinthians 10:4)

How often do you pull out your physical Bible in the heat of temptation? When the enemy whispers fearful lies into your ear, do you run and grab your Bible to have a random thirty-minute devotional? Most of us do not. Many times, when temptation strikes, we are not in a position to go look up certain verses in the Bible that will encourage us to stay on the straight and narrow path. And if we are honest, most of us would not even know where to look in our Bibles for a specific word, even if we were carrying a Bible at all times. This is another reason we must have Scripture tucked away in our hearts and minds. Temptations and fears come in the flash of a nanosecond with an aggressive and compelling voice. We need to have the sword of God ready within us to deflect these blows. When you have Scripture memorized, you can recall it in an instant and allow it to direct you back toward the Lord, no matter where you are or what time of day or night it is.

VICTORY STORY

Ben Wenger

Actor, Youth Ministry Leader,
Piercing Word Team Member

Over the last few years I have made Scripture memorization a routine practice in my devotional life. Memorizing Scripture has blessed me and has been a great encouragement in my walk with God. I've found that memorizing big passages of Scripture produces deep experiences of meditation, when those passages are engraved in my head through memorization, I can recall them at any time, on a long car drive or walk in the park or while I'm waiting for an appointment, and as I keep reciting those passages God reveals to me deeper truths. I'm still gleaning new insights from passages that I've meditated on for years. I've also found that memorizing Scripture has enhanced my prayer life, because it enables me to have a two-way conversation with God. I speak to him through prayer and he speaks to me through his Word. Memorizing Scripture has been a big help in fighting temptation. Behind every temptation is a lie, a lie that promises good outside of God. Memorizing Scripture enables me to have the promises of God close at hand to fight the lies of temptation.

Take the helmet of salvation, and the sword of the Spirit, which is the word of God. (Ephesians 6:17)

We are in a spiritual battle. How can we effectively fight this spiritual battle if we don't wield our sword ever-ready in our hand? You are in the midst of battle. Ready your sword!

Know and love Jesus more

Abide in me, and I in you. As the branch cannot bear fruit by itself, unless it abides in the vine, neither can you, unless you abide in me. (John 15:4)

How can we remain in love with our Savior if we do not continually read his love letters to us? In a marriage, if the spouses neglect to invest purposefully in their relationship, they may still remain married but the love relationship between them dies out. This kind of couple could probably not convince a single young person of how amazing marriage is, because they are not currently experiencing what true marriage should look and feel like.

Similarly, we may remain "married" to our heavenly Bridegroom but have fallen out of love with him. We will then be dull and ineffective when we attempt to share our faith, because the flame of passion for our Savior will have been reduced to a mere mental commitment to follow him.

We do not want to make light of this level of commitment in any way. Our current culture often lacks a respect for commitment, yet commitment is vital to the health of every marriage or partnership of any kind. However, even a committed marriage would be rather dull without love, joy, and passion. Oh, let us stir up our zeal for the Lord again! But how? How do you fall in love with another person? You get to know them. You become intimately acquainted with their likes and dislikes, their passions and opinions, their history and their hopes, their dreams and fears. You spend time with them, talk with them, exchange letters, share experiences, work together, laugh together—you get the idea.

VICTORY STORY

Steve Douglass

Emily's Father, WBYN Radio Station Sales Representative, Piercing Word Supporter

When I memorized (and re-memorized) the Sermon on the Mount passage, I found that many times one of the verses would come to my mind as I was going through my day. This was triggered by something I saw or experienced. It wasn't like I tried to think of a verse; it just came to my mind. Sometimes during a conversation, a verse or two would come to mind that was applicable to our conversation and I would share that verse with the person I was talking to. When the Word of God is memorized and meditated on, I truly experience it as the Living Word (see Luke 8:15).

Memorizing verses, chapters, and even whole books of the Bible is incredibly effective in our effort to know God more profoundly. This purposeful time in the Word will be like water and sunshine upon your relationship with Jesus. If you have been in a rut of simply reading the Bible for years and years, we strongly suggest you incorporate memorization alongside your reading as an ongoing spiritual discipline. You can change it up even more by replacing your Bible reading time with memorization for a season.

Let's get to know our Savior through his Word and through spending intimate times in his presence. Only then can we go out and change the world.

Become more like Christ

Do not be conformed to this world, but be transformed by the renewal of your mind, that by testing you may discern what is the will of God, what is good and acceptable and perfect. (Romans 12:2)

Jesus quoted Scripture in the desert, in the synagogue, on the streets, and even on the cross. If the Son of God memorized and quoted Scripture in times of need, how in the world do we think we can do otherwise? If Jesus needed to have scriptural truths tucked away in his heart and mind to deflect the lies of the enemy, how much more must we need them!

When we memorize God's truth, it changes us from the inside out and we become more like our Jesus. If we do not apply

> SWORDPLAY TIP
>
> **The more we soak in God's truth, the more our minds are transformed.**

the Scripture to our lives, what's the point of learning it in the first place? We must actually live out the Word or we, like the hypocritical Pharisees of Jesus's day, will become white-washed tombs, looking good on the outside but being dead on the inside. We cannot become more like Jesus by our own effort or striving. If we spend time with him and in the truth of his Word, we will find ourselves changed into his likeness by no power of our own, and we will grow more and more to have "the mind of Christ" (1 Corinthians 2:16).

Stand firm against the lies of the enemy

> See to it that no one takes you captive by philosophy and empty deceit, according to human tradition, according to the elemental spirits of the world, and not according to Christ. For in him the whole fullness of deity dwells bodily, and you have been filled in him, who is the head of all rule and authority. (Colossians 2:8–10)

We live in a culture that believes in relative truth. Lies are everywhere, cleverly masquerading as truth. Having the Word of God committed to memory will enable us to discern truth from lies in our culture, movies, books, teachings, blogs, and more.

In the biblical record of Jesus being tempted in the wilderness, we see Satan himself quoted Scripture, but in a twisted manner he meant to cunningly deceive. If the devil mangles Scripture in an attempt to swindle Christ-followers, it is imperative that we understand the context of Scripture so that we are not deceived by a wrong interpretation of God's Word. This is why we at Piercing Word are such big fans of memorizing whole chapters and books of the Bible and not just single verses. It is much easier to take a single verse out of context than it is an entire chapter or book. We need to know the Word of God better than the devil knows it.

The Victory Story on the next page is a powerful testimony of one girl's fight against the lies of the enemy.

Enhanced study of God's Word

> But as for you, continue in what you have learned and have firmly believed, knowing from whom you learned it and how from childhood you have been acquainted with the sacred writings, which are able to make you wise for salvation through faith in Christ Jesus. All Scripture is breathed out by God and profitable for teaching, for reproof, for correction, and for training in righteousness, that the man of God may be complete, equipped for every good work. (2 Timothy 3:14–17)

When you are intimately familiar with the Bible through memorization, it becomes that much easier to study other parts of Scripture because you can cross-reference in your head. The Bible is ultimately one

VICTORY STORY

Victoria Glick

Student, Dancer,
Former Piercing Word Intern

I think the biggest way God has impacted me through Scripture is a distinct moment that took place in the month of December. I was driving, and I had a panic attack. Leading up to this, Aaron had challenged me to memorize a gospel presentation as a part of my internship project. I had been struggling; the memorization was not easy for me. While I was having this panic attack, I remembered some advice my mentor had given me: to quote Scripture to ward off the lies of the enemy and the anxious feelings that were going on inside my mind. The only Scripture that came to my mind was the gospel presentation. So, reluctantly, I began to quote it to myself. The passage begins with "Now I would remind you brothers of the gospel" (1 Corinthians 15:1).

It was amazing for me to remind myself of God's truth—reminding myself that Christ has died for my sin and I am no longer a slave to Satan. I no longer belong to him because Christ has set me free. He has set me free from these panic attacks and the anxiety that I feel. It was really an incredible moment for me because a lot of my battles have been mental; it has been very helpful to have Scripture memorized that can equip me to fend off the lies of the enemy.

Previously, whenever I had a panic attack or started to overthink or have a mental breakdown, I would tell myself "I'm okay. I can do this. I can get through this." I relied on my own strength. And so this year, especially having to memorize Scripture in the Piercing Word internship, I have realized that I need to rely on God's strength. Only through memorizing and quoting Scripture have I been able to find lasting peace that comes without an explanation.

story, so the more we can know it as a whole instead of separating it into bite-sized pieces, the more we will understand God's big picture through his Word.

Both of us have personally experienced "light bulb" moments during sermons, Bible studies, or personal devotions where a passage is read that explains another passage we already have memorized. It is incredibly exciting to have these moments where the intricate web of God's Word intersects with itself.

It is also fascinating to compare different Bible translations with the memorized translation. Comparing and contrasting translations has never been easier than when you have one of them memorized already. The point of this exercise is not to pass judgment on another translation. On the contrary, different translations are helpful for giving us a fuller perspective of the actual meaning behind the Greek and Hebrew texts.

Memorizing large chunks of contextual Scripture will also be useful in evaluating the messages you hear from various teachers, pastors, or even friends expressing their opinions. Having a firm grasp on God's words is essential in differentiating false prophets or false teaching from the truth.

Preparation for end times

> Stay awake, for you do not know on what day your Lord is coming. But know this, that if the master of the house had known in what part of the night the thief was coming, he would have stayed awake and would not have let his house be broken into. Therefore you also must be ready, for the Son of Man is coming at an hour you do not expect. (Matthew 24:42–44)

We believe one of the reasons God called the ministry of Piercing Word into existence is to help prepare the church for the end times. We are so blessed to live in a country where, for the most part, we are granted religious freedom. However, we believe that the Bible makes it clear this will not always be the case. Many Christians in other countries are experiencing intense persecution for their faith. We believe that, someday, we will be among them. we do not say these things to make anyone afraid, but rather so that we can properly prepare. Part of preparing for religious persecution is hiding God's Word in our hearts. When persecution begins, usually one of the first things the perpetrators attempt is to eradicate the Word of God. They can steal physical paper from us, but they can never steal the truth we write on our hearts

SWORDPLAY TIP

Man cannot steal or burn away that which is written on our hearts and minds.

and minds. Just imagine—what if your entire church collectively memorized the New Testament together? What if you and your church collectively memorized the *entire Bible*? This way, the Word of God will not be lost, for it will be imprinted on our hearts and minds.

The Call for New Recruits

The spiritual battle is raging. Many people are falling to the attacks of the enemy, and many more will fall. Will you be one of them? Or will you learn how to stand up and fight? Will you learn how to wield the sword of the Spirit in spiritual combat? Will you discipline yourself and allow the Holy Spirit to change you from the inside out through the Word of God? Will you join us in becoming a warrior of the Word?

Your progress through the memorization process

☑ **KNOW WHY**

<u>Know How</u>
- ☐ Plan It
- ☐ Understand It
- ☐ See It, Say It, Do It
- ☐ Review It
- ☐ Apply It
- (Repeat)

WARRIOR TRAINING DRILL

1. List the three reasons for memorizing Scripture that resonate most with your heart:

   1. _____

   2. _____

   3. _____

2. Write a prayer to God about why you desire to know him through his Word on a deeper level by hiding it in your heart.

   _____

   _____

   _____

3. What are some specific ways you have seen God's Word aid you, both spiritually and practically?

   1. _____

   2. _____

   3. _____

4. Join the growing online community of Bible Memorizers by joining our Warriors of the Word Facebook Group! This is a group of fellow warriors and is meant to be a place to find and give encouragement and comradery, and to offer each other practical help along the way. Our Piercing Word Staff are also group members and are available to help troubleshoot and answer your questions as you walk forward in your Scripture memorization journey. Upon joining the page, introduce yourself by posting a selfie with your reason for becoming a Warrior of the Word. Simply post this phrase with your selfie photo and fill in the blank, "I am becoming a Warrior of the Word to win spiritual victory in the area of _____!" (ex. Lust, fear, pride, sharing the gospel with boldness, encouraging others, knowing God better, etc.)

CHAPTER 2

Welcome to Boot Camp

No Excuses!

In all circumstances take up . . . the sword of the Spirit,
which is the word of God, praying at all times in the Spirit, with all
prayer and supplication. ~ Ephesians 6:16–18

A Sheathed Sword

One day after a Piercing Word Scripture Performance, a high-schooler with brown hair and glasses came up to me at our information table in the lobby and meekly introduced himself as Aiden. As we talked, he confided, "a friend of mine doesn't believe that memorizing Scripture is important. What should I say to him?"

I replied, "If I were you, I would say to that friend, 'Do you believe that we are currently in a spiritual battle?'" He nodded as if he were role playing this supposed conversation with his friend. "And if we are, do you think it would be more valuable to have your sword in your hand or in your sheath while in action on the battlefield?"

"In my hand, of course," he replied.

"The Word of God on your smartphone app in your pocket or on the pages of your Bible back at home is a sheathed sword," I continued. "When you memorize and internalize the Word of God, suddenly

AARON

31

you have it in your hand, and you are ready to wield it against the schemes of the enemy. You are ready to fell your enemy or deflect his blows. A sheathed sword does no one any good except to make one look good to others and feel good. While it should feel good to have such a weapon at your hip, it should feel even better to have it in your hand. If it is in your hand, it could actually save your life and the lives of those around you. Sheathed swords never see battle and don't save lives. That is why I memorize Scripture. I realize that I am in a battle, and I must use the only offensive weapon God has given us against the enemy. I refuse to go into battle every day without having it in my hand, and so should you." Aiden thanked me for the conversation and walked away with a renewed perspective.

The Most Common Objections to Memorizing Scripture

If we are being honest, many of us would admit to having many unspoken objections to memorizing Scripture. Emily and I would like to take some time to address each of these common objections. Our goal in Boot Camp is to break down any barriers in your mind that may have been built up by the enemy and are keeping you from the vital spiritual discipline of Scripture memory.

I don't have a good memory.

I cannot tell you how many people I have met who have said to me, "I don't have a good memory." You may feel the same, but I can assure you that you *do* have a good memory. In fact, you have a incredible memory! David said in Psalm 139 that you are fearfully and wonderfully made, having been knit together in your mother's womb by God himself. In Genesis 1:26 we are told that we are made in the image of God. Your brain is more impressive and complex than the fastest supercomputers. You just need to learn how to operate it and train it to work hard for you. Maybe you have not been using this God-given resource well lately. That is okay! You can begin today to exercise your brain. It will grow stronger every day as you begin to use it for God's purposes.

I once attended a memorization seminar by Matthew Goerke. He has a memorization program called The Memory Switch, and he was very good at teaching various memorization techniques (though none of them were aimed at memorizing blocks of text like Scripture). At the beginning of the seminar, he asked the group, "How's your memory?" The immediate responses were "bad," "not good," or "okay." He then told us that one of the biggest pitfalls to memorization is our own lack of belief in our ability to memorize. He told us that anytime someone asks us how good our memory is, we should respond "Great!" Then he asked the group to remember a list of twenty items he quickly rattled off. No one was able to remember all of them. He asked us again, "How's your memory?" The group reluctantly responded, "Great."

As he continued the seminar, he taught some key techniques for memorizing lists using numerical and visual association. After successfully teaching us how to remember and recite back to him "The Tree List" as he called it, he asked us again, "How's your memory?" The group, amazed at what they had just been able to do, shouted wildly, "Great!" He ended the seminar shortly after that. I will never forget what I learned there. It is *so* true. Your own tongue can speak life or death into any part of your body or soul.

> Death and life are in the power of the tongue,
>> and those who love it will eat its fruits. (Proverbs 18:21)

Your faith in God and who he has made you to be will determine what you are able to do and not do. Chances are you have just as good of a brain as I do, if not better.

> SWORDPLAY TIP
>
> **Speak words of life over yourself.**

My brain doesn't work like it used to.

In the book *Moonwalking with Einstein*, Joshua Foer masterfully tells his own story of going from journalist to memorization expert in only one year. His story is both inspiring and insightful as he shows that pretty much anyone can succeed and even excel at memorization when using time-tested techniques. In this book, Foer shares how he met and talked with an aging memorization expert and coach, Tony Buzan, who candidly shares, "People assume that memory decline is a function of being human and therefore natural, but that is a logical error. Because normal is not necessarily natural."[1] Buzan then goes on to claim that his own memory has only improved every year with age. This may seem astounding. However, there are some simple and practical explanations as to how possible it is for any person to walk in this reality. Much of what it comes down to is discipline and good self-care.

"People assume that memory decline is a function of being human and therefore natural, but that is a logical error. Because normal is not necessarily natural." (Tony Buzan)

Our brains are not a library with a limited number of shelves to store information. Our brains operate more like a muscle that grows with use. If you go to the gym and work out vigorously for the first time in twenty years, you are going to be sore the next day. But if you stay consistent in going to the gym, your muscles will grow and get stronger with each passing day. The same goes for memorization. If you have not memorized anything in a while, it's probably going to hurt the first few times you get back into

VICTORY STORY

Paul Marini
Actor,
Piercing Word Team Member

When I started memorizing, I was very weak. I couldn't do very much memorization. But over the past couple of years, working with Piercing Word and doing it so much, I have developed a lot of mental strength. Now I can memorize larger portions in a much shorter amount of time; it is so much easier now because I have strengthened those memorization muscles. Memorizing Scripture for me has revolutionized my walk with God. It has changed so much. Memorization has become a part of my life now. The Holy Spirit brings up all these verses, chapters, and books at the right time and either speaks to me or uses them to speak to somebody else. One of the incredible things about God that just blows me away is the lengths to which he goes to communicate with us. In every single [Piercing Word] production I have been involved with, God has used a specific Scripture to speak to me, influence me, direct me, and help me grow.

it. However, if you are consistent with your memorization and review every day, your brain will get stronger and more able to retain the information you give it.

Another common misconception about our brains is that they should work well no matter how we treat them or what we feed them. Just as our bodies get fat and lazy if we only watch TV and eat potato chips, our brains are the same. If you only feed your body and brain junk food, you might just be starving your brain of what it needs to properly function and memorize. Generally speaking, your brain operates at a high level when it has the nutrition it needs to function well. For recommended resources on how to support healthy brain function and prevent neurological decay, please see section F of the Battle Resources in the back of this book.

Memorization is boring.

Is the Bible a boring book? I can almost see you vehemently shaking your head. Well then, if you are in a room alone with the Bible and you are bored, who is the boring one? The only person we have to blame for feelings of boredom is our own self. It is up to us to make memorization fun and engaging. The entire premise of this book is to help you replace boring memorization habits with fun-filled, life giving spiritual discipline. There is much about how to shift this perspective and practice in chapter 6, "The Art of War."

For now, let us give you an analogy that will help explain the essential difference in the two approaches of going about memorization:

> **SWORDPLAY TIP**
>
> God's Word is not boring. If you are bored while memorizing Scripture, you are doing it wrong.

the boring way and the fun way. The problem with the manner in which most people go about memorization is that they memorize a piece of text as if they were picking up a cardboard box of information one hundred times in a row and putting it back down in the same exact place. They literally read the text on the page over and over again in the same exact fashion in hopes that by the fiftieth or hundredth time, it will finally stick. Our brains see this as an incredibly boring and meaningless activity. When an activity is boring, it will

prove ineffective and unfruitful. If this is how most people attempt Scripture memorization, it is no wonder people avoid it.

The system we use to teach memorization is more like showing people how to open the box of information, remove the contents, examine them carefully, build something creative and interesting with the pieces, then throw the box away and place their new creation in a visible place in their mind. It is creative, productive, fascinating, beneficial, and insightful to memorize in such a fashion. This book will help you to learn how to memorize in this manner and be able to say goodbye to boring memorization.

I have the Bible in my pocket on my smartphone. I don't need to memorize it.

This is an excuse that most often resides, unspoken, in our subconscious. It is a blessing to have the Word of God so easily accessible. However, having easy access to the Bible is different than having it tucked away in your heart. It is not the words on the shelf or even the words in our mind that will change our lives and the lives of those around us—it is the words that have been planted deep in the soil of our hearts that will truly effect change. No wise warrior will charge into battle with his sword in its sheath. Similarly, we must have our spiritual sword "in hand," ready to instantly fight the flaming darts of the enemy.

In a world of externalized memories, where so much of our information is stored in books or on the internet instead of our brains, most of us not only don't know how to memorize but can't think of a single good reason to memorize anything. However, this world of externalized memories is a recent phenomenon. For the majority of human history, if you wanted to know something or remember something, you had to memorize it. Most written texts of the ancient world were written with the aim to aid memorization and recitation, as the majority of the people would only ever experience the text auditorily. Back then, the art of memorization was necessary to the human experience. Today, most people view it as completely unnecessary. In Joshua Foer's book entitled *Moonwalking with Einstein*, he addresses the importance of memory:

How we perceive the world and how we act in it are products of how and what we remember. We are all just a bundle of habits shaped by our memories. . . . Now more than ever, as the role of memory in our culture erodes faster than ever before, we need to cultivate our ability to remember. Our memories make us who we are. They are the seed of our values and source of our character. . . . Memory training is . . . about nurturing something profoundly and essentially human.[6]

If our memories make us who we are and are the seed of our values and source of our character, then we need to memorize the Bible.

> SWORDPLAY TIP
>
> It is not the words on the shelf that will change our lives and the lives of those around us, but the words that have been planted deep in the soil of our hearts.

My kids are too young to memorize Scripture.

You would be surprised how much children, even toddlers, can memorize. Our son, Caleb, memorized "Rejoice always" from 1 Thessalonians 5:16 when he was a rambunctious two year old and shortly after that memorized "Jesus wept." We have seen three- and four-year-old children successfully reciting a Bible verse for every letter of the alphabet. For specific challenges and ideas, see Children and Family Challenges in chapter 3. Also find our favorite list of ABC Bible Verses in section 1 of The Arsenal at the back of this book.

I'm too old.

In 2014, we met a ninety-four-year-old lady named Ellie on a Piercing Word tour through the New England states. She told us that she was half blind and nearly deaf. She had seen us perform Scripture the previous year and had taken our challenge to memorize an entire psalm. She had successfully memorized Psalm 91 that year. Praise the Lord! If Ellie can do it, you can too.

EMILY

On the other hand, cognitive decline is something that many people are faced with as they age. However, just because you can't memorize as well as you could when you were twenty, it doesn't mean you shouldn't memorize now. You may feel slow, but it is never impossible. It still honors God. You can say along with Paul, "I can do all things through Christ who strengthens me" (Philippians 4:13 [NKJV]).

VICTORY STORY

Beth Weaver

Senior Citizen, Former Overseas
Missionary, Piercing Word Supporter

Over fifty years ago, when I was in middle school, I began regular Bible memorization with BMA (Bible Memory Association). They had rewards to camp and books and other prizes, so all these were a great motivation to me when a child.

Now that I am older, I call memorization my "A.P.P." (that is, Alzheimer's Prevention Program). If you don't use it you lose it, or so they say. My favorite approach is putting 3 x 5 index cards on a ring holder that has a plastic cover and a built-in elastic band. The text only sinks into my well-seasoned brain if I'm moving. My favorite places to concentrate while moving are on the elliptical machine at the gym or on my favorite twelve-mile bicycle route. With the aid of the machinery rhythm, I often put the lines to music. I compose as I go.

I find my handy-dandy ring 3 x 5 card sets with the plastic cover and built-in elastic to hold it together at the Staples store. I then print the verses out in big and bold font so it's easier for me to see the words and flip through the cards as I work out. I was also once told that if you review a verse every day for thirty days in a row, you will never lose it.

I would encourage anyone to listen over and over again to the passage they wish to memorize. I use the YouVersion Bible on my smartphone. If I hear the text repeatedly, it becomes more intimate, making it easier to learn.

During our first eight years of missionary life in Haiti, I challenged my guitar students one summer to take our Vacation Bible School (VBS) verses and put them to music. I was so excited because just that week I had prayed for God to give me a tune to one of the verses. I assured the guitarists that God would want to give them tunes for each of the verses I assigned them. The next week, we recorded and played the songs over our Radio Lumiere Dame-Marie station so that the kids in our region had a head start on their memory verses before they even showed up at VBS.

I was recently asked to share how I use prayers from Scripture. I demonstrated by praying for our three daughters in front of the group by quoting prayers from Ephesians 1 and 3. I challenged these younger women to pray God's Word back to their Father in heaven . . . for their children.

God brings his Word back to my memory right when I need it for circumstances at hand. God's Word has guarded me and guided me over many years of ministry.

If you don't think it is possible to memorize God's Word at an older age, we hope you were inspired by Beth Weaver and her "Alzheimer's Prevention Program." Many of the memorization techniques in this book will aid you in becoming a kid again through using multiple learning styles and engaging your whole self to successfully hide God's Word in your heart.

I'm too busy to memorize Scripture.

We feel this sentiment often as we are currently in a stage of parenting two toddlers and a baby. It often seems that every moment is consumed by changing diapers, switching laundry, and kissing boo-boos. However, we would argue that we are too busy not to be meditating on and memorizing God's Word. Martin Luther has been an inspiration and challenge to us in this. One day, when a friend asked him about his plans for the following day, he replied, "Work, work from early until late. In fact, I have so much to do that I shall spend the first three hours in prayer."[2]

We find the busier we are, the more we are tempted to neglect God's Word. At the same time, the busier we are, the more we need God's Word reminding us of truth in everyday situations and difficulties.

This excuse feels valid in extremely busy seasons, such as the parenting stage. And yet it is imperative that we not only teach those under our care how to love God's Word themselves but that we set the example for them through our own personal habits with the Lord. For specific ideas on how to memorize even in a busy season, whether parenting or otherwise, see our section about On-the-Go Memorization Tactics for Life's Busy Seasons (Battle Resources: H).

VICTORY STORY

Caleb Hughes
Piercing Word
Artistic Director

I was a full-time student working a part-time job. Plus I was married. For me, if Bible memorization happened, it was at the end of the day while lying in bed . . . at least that's when I wanted it to happen. No matter how hard I tried, the heaviness of my eyelids always seemed greater than my determination to memorize. But amidst a busy day, an evening of homework, and time with my wife, what other options did I have?

Then I had a game-changing realization. Twice a day, I had fifteen minutes when I had to go outside. Any guesses as to why? Two words: golden retriever. Being the owner of a high-energy puppy meant that each day I had to take my dog outside to play. But other than the occasional throwing of the ball, I usually just stood and watched my dog run around and sniff the grass. Then it dawned on me that these fifteen uninterrupted minutes could be an ideal opportunity to redeem my memorization efforts. So I gave it a try.

I saw immediate improvement. Passages that I had been laboring over for weeks were suddenly in my grasp. No longer was I falling asleep mid-memorization, but I was actively retaining the words on the page. I had exchanged a mundane, ineffective, and forced experience for a more enjoyable (I'm a fan of the outdoors), natural, and effective one. And for someone who felt like they were too busy to memorize, this built-in routine became the perfect solution for my packed schedule.

I am afraid of failing. What if I don't reach my memorization goal?

We have good news for you; you cannot fail at memorizing Scripture. We believe that this is one of Satan's strategies for keeping us from memorizing God's Word. Fear of failure is a strong anxiety for many people. Often, we do not believe we can succeed or do it as perfectly as we desire, so we deem it better to not even start. What a lie from hell! You cannot fail at memorizing Scripture because no matter what, even if you do not finish, you will have more Scripture in your heart than before. This means that you cannot lose when memorizing God's Word. It is a *win* every time. Even if not a single word sticks in your brain (which is unlikely) you will have spent time meditating on God's truth. That alone will refresh and change your mind and heart.

> **SWORDPLAY TIP**
>
> **You cannot fail at memorizing Scripture because, no matter what, you will have more Scripture in your heart than before.**

It scares me to think of reciting what I have tried to memorize. I'm afraid of being humiliated.

Some people are afraid to take the leap of memorizing Scripture because they are afraid of humiliation. This is often a subconscious feeling that one might have trouble even expressing verbally. Often, this person has had a frightening experience connected with memorization in his or her past.

This was the case of a sweet lady in her eighties who took part in a Bible memorization class we hosted at our church. We assigned her specific verses to memorize and recite at the end of the seven-week class. She came up to us afterward, expressing mild terror at the thought of reciting her verses in front of a bunch of people. Then this dear woman relayed a story from when she was in a play in elementary school and she blanked on one of her lines while on stage. Seventy-some years later, she was still frozen in fear. We had the privilege of walking alongside her for a season in her memorization journey and watch her courageously persevere.

Many of us can relate to this story more than we would like to admit. The key to this is to move past fear—to give your fear to the Lord and, in daring faith, step forward in memorizing his Word. Don't allow the devil to have a victory in your spiritual life because of a fearful past experience. Tell yourself the truth that God already sees

VICTORY STORY

Priscilla Hodecker
Senior Citizen, Women's Ministry Leader, Piercing Word Supporter

My absolute most precious possession in this whole world is the Word of God, his presence in my life, and his promise of eternal life. Absolutely nothing is more important to me. Being intentional to memorize the Word is an act of worship for me. It is humbling that I am able to feed my own spirit while memorizing, because Jesus says, "the words that I speak to you are spirit, and they are life"(John 6:63 [NKJV]). Since God's Word equals the truth and sets me free (John 8:32), it is worth my time, effort, and diligence to memorize.

I find it amazing how many moments during any given day can be used to work on memorizing God's Word when there is a goal. I have the given passage typed out and ready to take with me to the gym, carry on a brisk walk or when driving, read when washing dishes, work on with someone else (even grandchildren), or review when being quiet before I fall asleep. Repeating the Word of God out loud is crucial and helps me maintain focus. Listening to the passage using a Bible app also aids in the process.

Having the Word of God at my disposal when conversing with family, friends, and unbelievers gives me confidence to speak the Word of Truth and enriches my prayers on their behalf. Now in my seventies, I am finding it takes longer and is a bit harder to recite verses exactly, but by faith I am sure my spirit is being nourished, transformed, and will bear forth fruit for the kingdom of God and into eternity.

you as *enough*, that Christ is your victory, and that you are precious in God's sight.

It never occurred to me to memorize more than individual verses of the Bible.

This is true for many people. It had never occurred to me to memorize an entire book of the Bible until I met Aaron. I didn't know anyone else who had done that. Memorizing verses is a wonderful thing, but I discovered such beauty and spiritual depth in memorizing an entire chapter, book, or even just a defined passage. I have tasted this extra richness as I come to understand the greater context of what I'm memorizing. Healthy methods of memorization should always include contextual study of the passage. In fact, effective memorization necessitates meditation. Repeating the passage over and over, saying it with different inflections, contemplating its meaning, researching its historical context, praying about how to personally apply it—these all are ways of meditating on a truth. Memorization drives us to meditation and study, and therefore gives us a much fuller understanding of the truth of what we are memorizing, more than simply reading it in context can do.

Boot Camp Wrap-Up

Now that these excuses have been brought into the light, it's time to deal with them. Your Warrior Training Drills at the end of this section will help you specifically identify any of your own personal excuses. Then you will have an opportunity to spend some time confessing to the Lord any attitudes and excuses that have kept you from wielding the sword of the Spirit. This is where your battle begins.

1. What excuses, lies, or fears have been keeping you from memorizing God's Word? Write them here.

   _____

   _____

2. Find one Scripture that specifically combats each excuse, lie, or fear and write it here.

   _____

   _____

3. Write a prayer of confession to God for any attitudes or excuses that have kept you from spending time in his Word.

   _____

   _____

   _____

   _____

4. Talk positively to yourself. Tell yourself that you *can* do it, you *are able to memorize.* We can either build ourselves up or tear ourselves down with our words. Let's speak God's truth over ourselves instead of an earthly lie that we have embraced. God's truth is that:

   "Nothing will be impossible with God" (Luke 1:37)

   "Is anything too hard for Me?" (Jeremiah 32:27)

   "I can do everything through Christ, who gives me strength." (Philippians 4:13 NLT)

   Speak these verses over yourself this week as you prepare to memorize God's Word.

5. Log in to the Warriors of the Word Facebook Group and encourage someone else who has recently posted.

CHAPTER 3
Select Your Weapon
Picking a Passage

The word of God is living and active, sharper than any two-edged sword, piercing to the division of soul and of spirit, of joints and of marrow, and discerning the thoughts and intentions of the heart.
~ Hebrews 4:12

A Reluctant Warrior

If you had asked me as a child or teenager if I enjoyed memorization, I would have told you I hated it. The word "memorization" reminded me of the boring lists of people, places, dates, and mathematical formulas I was expected to remember in order to do well on tests. These lists frustrated me and never seemed to stick in my memory.

However, as I look back, I realize there were many things I did remember successfully and even enjoyed memorizing, such as Scripture with my family, skip counting, prepositional phrases, and the many countries of Africa. Back then, I was not able to analyze why I could memorize and even enjoy memorizing some things more successfully than others.

Now I do understand. When homeschooling, my mom led us kids in creating memorable hand motions for each phrase as we memorized parts of the Sermon on the Mount. Every number we skip-counted

EMILY

came with a catchy tune, and prepositional phrases were made into a rhythmic chant over which my siblings and I competed for perfection. In geography, each country in Africa became a character or "prop" in a complex plot my imagination crafted as I studied the colorful map spread across my lap.

It is now clear to me that I did indeed know ways to make memorization engaging and fun. But I wasn't able to break it down and apply the methods to other things that I wanted or needed to memorize.

My attitude about memorization—that I hated it—was probably the reason I hardly attempted memorizing anything but single verses or short clusters of verses in the Bible. Even when I memorized verses, I found it hard to remember their references. That made review difficult because I couldn't remember where the verses were found. So, because I struggled to review a mere handful of verses, the idea of memorizing an entire book of the Bible simply never occurred to me.

Fast forward to about a year after I graduated from high school. I took an incredible nine-month internship at a place called Gateway House of Prayer, a barn converted to a sanctuary, that is open to the community 24/7 for the purpose of prayer and communion with God. As part of my internship, we were required to memorize nearly two full chapters of 1 Corinthians. I had never memorized such a large chunk of Scripture, but because it was required, I plunged in. And do you know what? It wasn't as hard as I assumed it would be. I went on from there to memorize Psalm 27, which has remained a beloved friend that I run to during times of fear.

Fast forward again to age twenty-three. I was falling hard for my new friend, a passionate young man with a sandy beard, sea-swept eyes, and an infectious laugh. Aaron and I weren't yet dating at the time, but we shared similar passions: ministry and acting.

One day my phone rang and Aaron was on the other line with an unexpected request. Would I memorize the book of James with him and perform it for a local church? I hesitated for just a moment—I had never memorized anything so long. But how could I say "no" to the opportunity to hide God's Word in my heart? After all, I had now successfully memorized full chapters of Scripture. So I said yes and set myself to the task. Once again, it was not as hard as I had built it up in my mind to be. Certainly, it took much effort and required consistent practice. But in four or five weeks I had all five chapters memorized (*and* I had a new boyfriend). The beautiful book of James, as well as the incredible man I studied it with, grew nearer and dearer to my heart.

I share all of this with you to illustrate one major truth: Scripture memorization is a *journey.* Just like me, most of us do not go instantly from hating memorization to suddenly memorizing full books of the Bible. It is a personal journey that we each must take step by step. As you take each step forward, you gain a little more courage, and a little more, and a little more. Although I'm not sure I yet realized it, my step forward in memorizing an entire book of the Bible did not mean I had arrived at the end of my memorization journey. In fact, it was just the beginning—the beginning of a journey closer to the heart of God.

Selecting Your Weapon

When was the last time a passage from God's Word brought tears to your eyes or forced you to your knees before him? What Bible verses first helped you understand the gospel of Jesus Christ? What promises from his Word have you clung to in hard seasons of life? These are the places in the Bible we are going to look first as you endeavor to choose your spiritual weapons to wield against the enemy.

EMILY

The first entire book of the Bible I memorized was Philippians, and it has continued to be the most impactful. When it comes to picking a passage to memorize, you need to consider what God has taught you and what he is teaching you now. What are the most profound truths you have learned? What Bible passage is the Lord using to speak to you right now? Hopefully, as I ask these questions, specific passages are already coming to your mind. These are the passages you want to memorize first. These are the ones that will have the biggest effect on you as you continue to meditate on them for years to come.

If it has been a number of years since you memorized anything, you will want to start small. That is why we have structured our memorization challenges from small to large. No matter where you are on your memorization journey, you can jump into memorizing

God's Word intentionally and know what to memorize now and why. Also, many of the challenges we give in this chapter can be easily customized to suit your own situation. Clearly, "All Scripture is breathed out by God and profitable for teaching, for reproof, for correction, and for training in righteousness, that the man of God may be complete, equipped for every good work" (2 Timothy 3:16–17). That is why we have tried not to dictate too many specific passages, but rather help guide your own selections.

> **SWORDPLAY TIP**
>
> **No matter where you are on your Bible memorization journey, you can jump into memorizing God's Word intentionally now.**

In this book, we have included a number of suggestions about places to start memorizing Scripture. We have tied a strong reason to each passage suggested.

This is because we do not want you to memorize for the sake of memorizing or for the sake of pride. We want you to memorize Scripture in order to *know God better* and *apply* the truths of God's Word in your thoughts, emotions, beliefs, and actions. We want you to memorize the passages that will have the biggest effect on your current situations. In order to make your selection easier, we have divided the various individual memorization challenges into levels:

Essentials Track (Beginner)
Growing Track (Early Intermediate)
Sharing Track (Intermediate)
Knowing Track (Advanced)

Let's think back to some of the reasons we should memorize Scripture. These reasons have shaped the different memorization tracks and have formed our personal beliefs and teachings on memorizing Scripture over the years. Anytime we give a workshop and ask people to share reasons why they think they should memorize Scripture, someone will inevitably reply, "that I might not sin against thee" from Psalm 119:11(KJV). Other common answers are "to share your faith," or "to give a reason for the hope that is in you." These are good reasons. But does every verse in the Bible help you to fight temptation? The correct answer is no. For instance, if you memorized Exodus 28:5, "They shall receive gold, blue and purple and scarlet yarns, and fine twined linen," that verse is not going to do you a lick of good in a situation when you are tempted. Or if you memorized Genesis 10:26, "Joktan fathered Almodad, Sheleph, Hazarmaveth, Jerah," would that verse aid you in sharing your faith in Jesus Christ with an unbeliever? Probably not.

This is why we must be intentional when memorizing God's Word. Yes, "All Scripture is breathed out by God and profitable for teaching, for reproof, for correction, and for training in righteousness" (2 Timothy 3:16). However, each Scripture passage is effective for specific purposes. There are generally certain types of passages that everyone should prioritize in memorization more than others, such as gospel-centered passages versus an isolated genealogy list. However, the prioritization process will be somewhat different for each Christ-follower because each person's unique struggles, scenarios, and seasons will require a different Bible memorization focus. That is why the Bible Memorization Tracks in this chapter prioritize the types of Bible passages everyone should focus on first, while allowing for flexibility and personalization within each track.

> **SWORDPLAY TIP**
>
> **Each Scripture passage is effective for specific purposes.**

After explaining some personal memorization challenges for each track, we will give special and specific challenges for parents, children, pastors, small groups, and churches. These are opportunities for you to dream big and choose your next Bible passage to memorize as we *"spur one another on to love and good works"* (*Hebrews 10:24*).

Essentials Track (Beginner)

The Essentials Track is like your personal dagger that you can carry with you onto the spiritual battlefield. It is a small, attainable memorization challenge. It starts with memorizing one life verse, then five gospel verses and five to seven temptation or fear-fighter verses —in total, ten to twelve single verses. If you only do the Essentials Track, you will be light years ahead of many other believers. And you will begin to discover the immense power and effectiveness of the Word when wielded well on the spiritual battlefield of your mind, heart, and relationships.

1. Life verse

My life verse is Philippians 3:8. "I count everything as loss because of the surpassing worth of knowing Christ Jesus, my Lord." Philippians 3 has recentered me many times and the reference is even engraved on the inside of my wedding ring. It reminds me often that life is about knowing him and nothing else matters. Through this truth, I have learned how not to put my identity in anything except Christ. I am continually reminded of this when my soul tries to find its identity in anything but Christ.

Hopefully, selecting your life verse will be easy, as it should be a verse that has already profoundly touched you. It should be a passage that brings you back to the centrality of the gospel and that affects you daily. If you would like some suggestions, we have compiled a list of strong life verse options in section 3 of The Arsenal in the back of the book.

2. Gospel verses

The importance of memorizing gospel verses cannot be emphasized enough. Consider the Great Commission (Matthew 28:19–20). The reason this is the second challenge and not the first is because if you are not personally centered in your own knowing of God and your own identity in him, then you will be unable to share the gospel with others anyway. One of the simplest and easiest ways to be prepared to share the gospel at all times is by memorizing the "Romans Road," a popular grouping of verses from Paul's Epistle to the Romans:

> **SWORDPLAY TIP**
> **One of the simplest and easiest ways to be prepared to share the gospel at all times is memorizing the "Romans Road."**

Romans 3:23
Romans 6:23
Romans 5:8
Romans 10:9–10
Romans 10:13

This is a concise and clear gospel message. We have included the full text of these verses in section 4 of The Arsenal.

Another approach to being prepared with the gospel at all times is to memorize five verses that present the essential points of the gospel. In order to help you do this, we have created a Build-Your-Own Five-Verse Gospel Presentation Worksheet in section 5 of The Arsenal. This will help you build your own gospel presentation based on verses that resonate most strongly with you and your own story of reconciliation to God.

Whichever five gospel verses you end up choosing, these verses will be *essential* to you as you seek out opportunities to share your faith in Jesus Christ with people you encounter. Being able to tell someone exactly what the Bible says is far more persuasive than saying, "I think the Bible says something like . . ." Knowing these verses will equip you to be able to share your faith and do it well.

VICTORY STORY

Michael Lapham
Professional Actor,
Piercing Word Board Member

I like memorizing Scripture that aids my here and now—Scriptures about God's heart, man's sin, salvation in Jesus, and man's need for God's mercy and grace. My favorite times using Scripture have been in my personal witness to strangers or with people who are seeking to know more about Jesus. Without a doubt, leading people to Jesus has been my greatest encouragement and joy in my kingdom walk. If you haven't yet led someone to Jesus, then read your Bible, live the life Christ exemplified, and make disciples of men. Don't just memorize the Scriptures that will lead your faith to personal gain or prosperity, but memorize Scriptures that will lead you into the humble sacrifice of your life for God's purpose and for that of the world he loves. We are here to give, not to get. We who lay down our lives for the gospel will find great gain in God's everyday provision and peace.

3. Temptation fighter and fear fighter verses

Third, when choosing passages to memorize, you should consider your current struggles with the enemy—your temptations, fears, negative thoughts, and sinful tendencies. These need to be rooted out of your life as quickly as possible. How do you expect to fight the father of lies (see John 8:44) without the Word of God? The Word of Christ is the sword that proceeds from his mouth at the end of days to slay all his enemies (see Revelation 19:15). And you can defeat Satan with God's Word. Satan is out to steal, kill, and destroy (see John 10:10). You better be ready to fight when he comes knocking!

> SWORDPLAY TIP
>
> **When choosing a passage to memorize, pick Scriptures that target your current issues or struggles.**

I want to share with you a personal Victory Story about how I have used temptation fighter verses. I know this fight against temptation on an intimate level because I have wielded temptation fighters in my own battle against lust, one of the biggest giants on the spiritual battlefield.

When I was younger, I struggled with pornography. This struggle with lust made me painfully aware of my sinful nature before God. Surprisingly enough, it began during a season when I was spending consistent time with the Lord every morning. I wept before the Lord with conviction many times and prayed for the Lord to take my lust problem away. But Satan's battle schemes are usually more complex than that. I only began to see victory in this area when I opened up about this problem to some other guys and confessed my sin to them. At that point, I began having a regular accountability partner. I memorized some temptation fighter verses and put up strict internet boundaries for myself.

When I was confronted with a risqué image on an advertisement in the mall, I would quickly bounce my eyes and quote silently, "The body is not meant for sexual immorality, but for the Lord, and the Lord for the body." (1 Corinthians 6:13) God and I won many victories together with his Word as my sword. I fought hard but did not always win. Sometimes my flesh would get the better of me; I would lay down my sword and let the enemy slice me through.

When I began dating Emily, I had just begun a renewed effort to beat the enemy of lust by getting a new accountability partner, rememorizing my temptation fighter verses, putting up strict internet boundaries for myself, and praying intentionally for freedom and deliverance. One day, I told Emily about my struggle. Tears of hurt, pain, and betrayal filled her eyes. And I saw the truth: my "secret" sin was not just hurting me and my relationship with the Lord. It was injuring the person I loved most. I vowed that I never wanted to see that look in Emily's eyes again. God used that resolve to give me the strength I needed to push through the stranglehold of lust and into a place of total freedom in this area. Freedom is so good and is worth fighting for. It is for freedom that Christ has set us free (see Galatians 5:1).

This of course does not mean that I am never tempted to lust. In this over-sexed culture, we must always be on guard, no matter how many years we have been pure. It is often when we feel comfortable and confident in our freedom that we lay down our weapons and the enemy makes a surprise attack.

Because of this fact, I still keep my temptation fighters by my side, ready to use. I always make sure I have a consistent accountability partner. I still have strict internet boundaries, such as not allowing myself to go on the internet if I am awake after Emily goes to bed. I still make a habit of bouncing my eyes away from sensual images on billboards and advertisements that inadvertently cross my sight path. Temptation fighters have played an essential role in my fight for purity and continue to empower me to set my gaze on Christ in any surprise attack of temptation.

Temptation fighters are the third most essential type of Scripture passage to memorize. These will be different for everyone. We encourage you to seek out the verses that apply to your own specific struggles. As an example of what this can look like for you, see section 7 of The Arsenal, where Emily and I share some fighter verses we have used in the past to combat fear and lust respectively.

Also, The Navigators has come up with an amazing Topical Memory System with selected verses that address a number of different life issues. This is a great resource to look at if you are trying to find good temptation fighters for your own struggles. But even that resource is not exhaustive; there are plenty more areas of sin and struggle. Here is how we recommend searching for appropriate passages to fight your own biggest temptations, fears, and sin struggles.

1. Do a word search for your specific sin struggle or temptation at BibleGateway.com or in a Bible application on your phone. We enjoy using the ESV Bible app by Crossway for this purpose. Try to use synonyms if you don't find enough on your first search. You can also try searching for the opposite of your struggle. For instance, to find verses that combat greed you can search for "greed" or you can search for "contentment" or "content."

2. If an overwhelming number of verses come up in your search results, you may find applicable verses more quickly by starting your search in the New Testament. If you still need help, ask a pastor, teacher, parent, friend, or accountability partner for suggested verses to memorize on the subject.

3. Write the passages that resonate with you the most in your Bible Memorization Marching Orders in the back of this book (Battle Resources: A). You can also write them in a journal or on your phone where you can easily access them. Some great smart phone apps that you can use for typing, memorizing, and reviewing your chosen Bible verses are VerseLocker, Fighter Verses, and The Bible Memory App.

Searching for passages in the order we have listed above means you will be doing some personal digging before going to another resource for suggestions, which is the most beneficial strategy. If you find it yourself, you will likely end up reading more Scripture as you search (as well as more scriptural context) and therefore will grow more spiritually. However, we have also provided some resources for you in section 7 of The Arsenal to help you.

If you are still stuck and need help, you can always contact us at www.piercingword.org/contact. We would love to pray for you and help guide you along this path to knowing and wielding God's Word. Also, if you have additional resources that are not listed in this book, we would love to know about them. Please don't hesitate to send us a message. Your resource might just be added into later editions.

Growing Track (Early Intermediate)

The Growing Track will take you from memorizing single verses into memorizing short passages, sections, and chapters of the Bible. This is the place where your Bible memorization will increasingly grow your relationship and walk with Jesus. Here are some easy ways to begin that journey.

1. Three-verse challenge

In 2017, Piercing Word launched the three-verse challenge in an effort to flood the internet with the Word of God. The challenge is to memorize three consecutive verses, take a video of yourself reciting those verses, and post it to your social media pages with the hashtag #3versechallenge. It was exciting to witness Jesus-followers who hadn't memorized Scripture in years quote God's Word from their hearts. The challenge even spread to other parts of the world as our friends tagged their friends. We love to continue to challenge people with the three -verse challenge.

To participate, select three consecutive Bible verses to memorize. We recommend choosing a verse you already know and love, such as your life verse, and memorizing the verses surrounding it. You can either memorize the verse before and the verse after, or the two verses before, or the two verses after. After you memorize your verses and video yourself, tag and challenge three of your friends to do the same when you post it to social media. One of the reasons I love this challenge is because it is attainable for anyone, and has the potential to go viral if your friends take you up on it. It also helps you memorize and understand the context around a verse you have already memorized. And it is a challenge that is easy to share. We believe that just a handful of memorized verses can have a profound influence on your life and walk with Christ. So take the plunge, and begin your journey of going beyond the memorization of single verses.

Howie Zeager
Businessman, Small Group
Leader, Piercing Word Supporter

VICTORY STORY

When I was challenged with the #3versechallenge, at first I was like, "Eh, it's going to take me too long to do this." But I'm like, "Okay I'm going to memorize something." It has been a long time since I've memorized anything out of the Bible—maybe twenty years since I memorized anything word for word.

For this challenge, I memorized John 14:25–27 where Jesus was talking to his disciples. I think I was challenged to do it in twenty-four hours, but it took me two weeks, probably three or four hours total time just working on it every day. Even so, the experience was so worth it because I was repeating a promise that Jesus gave us and it really spoke to me. At first it was memorization. I just really tried to memorize. But as I came through it, I realized it wasn't just memorization. The promise became so real to me; it's amazing what happens when you repeat truth like that every day. "I say these things to you now, while I am still with you. But when the Father sends the Advocate as my representative, that is the Holy Spirit, he will teach you everything and remind you of everything I have told you. And I leave you with a gift, peace of mind and heart, and the peace I give is a gift that the world cannot give, so don't be troubled or afraid."

The #3versechallenge was so rewarding. I'm going to put the effort forth to memorize more verses, just simply to know my Heavenly Father better.

2. Psalm-of-your-age challenge

The psalm-of-your-age challenge is a fun way to memorize an entire chapter of Scripture, especially for those who have only memorized individual verses in the past. Look up the psalm that corresponds to your current age and memorize it. For example, if you are thirty-four years old, look up Psalm 34 and memorize it.

One of the reasons we love the psalm-of-your-age challenge is that it renews every year, and most psalms are between eight to thirteen verses, which is shorter than the average length of other chapters in the Bible. Psalms are also easy to relate to, which makes them easy to memorize for beginners.

3. Favorite-chapter challenge

Next, memorize your favorite chapter. This chapter may even include your life verse, which you have already memorized. If you do not have a favorite chapter, you may steal mine—Philippians 3, which is all about knowing Christ. A lot of people love Philippians 4 as well. Emily's favorite chapter is Isaiah 58 about true fasting. Romans 8 is one of the most beloved chapters in the Bible and one we highly recommend. James 1, Matthew 6, and 2 Peter 1 are also fantastic. If you do not already have a favorite chapter, read through some of these to see if one of them resonates strongly with you.

If you are intimidated by the thought of memorizing an entire chapter of the Bible, let me tell you that all it takes is memorizing one new verse a day for a month. Most chapters are about thirty verses long or less. You can go beyond what you think is possible. The plans and techniques in this book will show you how attainable it is to memorize one new verse every day for a month and memorize an entire chapter of God's Word. On the next page, read an amazing testimony about how memorizing an entire chapter like Romans 8 can turn tragedy into triumph in the spiritual realm.

Sharing Track (Intermediate)

The Sharing Track is exciting because it is primarily focused on memorizing passages for the purpose of encouraging others. In this track, you will experience the power of sharing Bible passages you have memorized as you pray over people, relay Bible stories, and articulate the gospel.

VICTORY STORY

Sharon Hartsough

Senior Citizen, Mother of Two,
Piercing Word Supporter

In December 2013, my sister invited me to Calvary Church to hear Piercing Word perform the Christmas story word for word from Scripture. I attended the performance and was inspired again to get my little cards out and memorize Romans chapter 8. I made up these little cards with the thirty-nine verses, and when I would go for walks or ride in the car, I could look at these and work at memorizing the verses.

On September 14, 2014, at 9:30 p.m., we received a phone call. A police officer was on the other end of the line. He asked if we could come and stay with our grandson, as his father had just died in a motorcycle accident. I said to the police officer, "That would be our son." He said, "Yes, ma'am." A few days later when I went to the funeral home to say my goodbyes, the pastor and I were the only ones in the room. He asked me if I would like to pray and I said, "Yes." I took my son's face in my hands, and the words that came out of my mouth were, "He who raised Christ Jesus from the dead will also give life to your mortal bodies through his Spirit who dwells in you" [Romans 8:11]. At that moment I felt peace and the radiant glory of God filling that room. By obeying God's command to hide God's Word in my heart, God took a moment of tragedy and turned it into a moment of triumph. His promises are for all who believe and God has promised that his Word will not return void. By memorizing God's Word, he has met my greatest need. He will do the same for you.

1. Prayers of the Bible

Certain prayers in the Bible are beneficial to know by heart and provide a meaningful study on how to pray. Once we have memorized these biblical prayers, we can mimic the heart of these prayers in our own praying. We can also pray these passages verbatim or personalize the prayers by replacing pronouns with names of people we are praying for, which is particularly influential. This can be done while praying alone, when praying over a friend or family member, or when praying in a group setting. Biblical prayers to read and consider memorizing are listed in section 8 of The Arsenal.

Emily and I have been profoundly stirred by the book *Face to Face, Volume 1: Praying the Scriptures for Intimate Worship* by Kenneth Boa. It is a daily devotional prayer guide that helps you pray the Scriptures for intimate worship. In this book, Kenneth leads the reader through praying the Scriptures and praying in accordance with them. The majority of the text is taken directly from the Bible, though he sometimes changes pronouns to help personalize the prayers. Kenneth takes the reader through the different types of prayer for each day with specific passages for each one: thanksgiving, confession, intercession, supplication, and so on. We highly recommend *Face to Face*. Consider using it in your personal times with the Lord.

2. Tellable Bible Stories

One day, while I was working in the Piercing Word office, I received a surprise visit by a tall energetic man who introduced himself as Larry Dinkins, missionary to Thailand. Larry told me that he is a certified instructor for Simply The Story, an organization that has created an entire discipleship curriculum based on the concept of teaching students to memorize 296 Bible stories. Here's the kicker: Simply The Story runs their discipleship schools in foreign countries where the majority of their Bible students are nonliterate. They memorize these stories by hearing them and repeating them back to the instructor until they can tell the story accurately, without missing important details. They do not drill down to ensure word-for-word retention. Rather, they ensure the Bible stories are told with 100 percent content accuracy but in their own words using normal speech. So if the students use synonyms for certain words or a proper name instead of a pronoun, their retelling would still get an A+, as long as all the details of the story remained intact. Larry even went so far as to say that these largely non-literate students were often more biblically adept and equipped for discipleship and ministry than many seminary graduates that he knew.

Larry explained, "A question I often ask of believers is 'Can you tell me a Bible story?' I have been amazed to find that few believers can repeat to me a Bible story accurately. Some are able to craft or summarize a short story from the Bible, but few can tell even one Bible story with content accuracy." Accurate knowledge of the Word and the ability to share and discuss it with others is simple and dynamic.

During that meeting, Larry described to me the basic memorization methodology used by Simply The Story. They use more of a thought-for-thought memorization method, which I will explain in more detail in chapter 9. Larry advocates what he calls "Optimum Bible Stories." These are stand-alone Bible stories that are fewer than fifteen verses long. They are action-oriented, visual, and contain minimal dialogue so they are easy to remember. Storytellers are encouraged to start with whichever Optimum Bible Stories resonate most with them personally.

Bible stories are power-packed, and they are often neglected when it comes to Bible memorization. Jesus used stories and parables extensively in his teaching. In fact, Matthew 13:34 tells us, "He said nothing to them without a parable." Memorizing Bible stories is an incredible way to get into God's Word and share stories of truth as Jesus did.

> **SWORDPLAY TIP**
>
> **Bible stories are power-packed, and they are often neglected when it comes to Bible memorization.**

Memorizing stories is an area Emily and I are currently trying to improve in. We want to be able to share Bible stories with our children as easily as if we were simply breathing. But Bible stories are not just for kids. In Kendall Haven's book entitled *Story Proof*, the author explores the effect of stories on the human brain from a scientific perspective. As he unpacks the power of story, he addresses cultural lies that we have come to believe about stories in regard to age. He says:

> We often falsely believe that stories are for children. Nonstories (factual articles, essays, data, and information) are for adults. Thus many unconsciously assume that

all stories look like children's stories. . . . As soon as a child grows old enough, they should set stories aside and move into the factual, truthful adult world of nonfiction and non-story. So, stories have been sidetracked into the kiddy corner and labeled, "just for fun." We believe that story is the opposite of logic, that stories aren't effective for conveying serious and important concepts. And without ever consciously pausing to consider either the veracity or implications of our assumptions, we set aside the most powerful communications and teaching tool available to humans and then idly wonder why our efforts to communicate to teach concepts, ideas, beliefs, values, attitudes, and facts do not succeed.[3]

I believe these statements to be terrifying and shockingly true. My friend Larry Dinkins emphasized to me, "All of us have encountered people who feel Bible stories are only for children, fun, and entertainment. They relegate storytelling to organizations like Child Evangelism Fellowship. Simply The Story has substantiated the power of our approach with children, but we must show that the stories in the Bible were primarily designed for adults and are suitable for deep inductive Bible study."

No matter what age you are, Bible stories are an invaluable teaching tool. Get ready to unlock the power of telling Bible stories as you include it in your Bible memorization Plan of Attack.

SWORDPLAY TIP

No matter what age you are, Bible stories are an invaluable teaching tool.

We have included a list of one hundred and ten tellable Bible stories in section 10 of The Arsenal. Let this resource help you decide which short Bible story you will memorize first. Be sure to start with a shorter Bible story and work your way up to longer Bible stories. Larry told me that even oral learners who are used to memorizing find it difficult to memorize stories that are over fifteen verses long. As you become accustomed to memorizing more and more short Bible stories, you can then expand to committing the longer ones to memory.

3. Five-minute gospel presentation:

At this point, you have already selected five gospel verses to take along with you as you share your faith with others one on one. But what if you had the opportunity to share the gospel with a group of people or from the stage? At Piercing Word, we do this all the time, and we have compiled a number of gospel verses together for this very purpose. We have several different gospel presentations that are all taken word for word from the ESV Bible.

In section 6 of The Arsenal, we have supplied you with a five-minute, seamless gospel presentation that is word for word from the ESV Bible. You can use this from the stage when giving an invitation to receive Jesus Christ. God has already used this exact gospel presentation to bring people into his kingdom. May he move mightily as you use it to share the gospel with others!

Knowing Track (Advanced)

This track gets at the heart of why I attempted to memorize the entire New Testament. I wanted to "know him" (Philippians 3:10). It is one thing to be equipped to survive on the spiritual battlefield (Essentials Track). It is another thing to be growing in your walk and relationship with the Lord (Growing Track) or be able to share Scripture with others (Sharing Track). It is an altogether sweeter and more profound thing to truly pursue knowing him (Knowing Track). Knowing his heart and desires, his moods, his pulse, his ups, his downs. Knowing what he likes and dislikes. Knowing what he cares about and what he doesn't care about. Knowing his quirks, his inconceivable and sometimes ironic oddities, his inexpressible beauty and grace and unsurpassable wisdom. This is the goal of the Knowing Track. In it, we move beyond the immediately practical verses and chapters into memorizing large passages and entire books of the Bible. Some of the verses within these passages and books may not have immediate surface application to our lives, but they *all* help us understand and know him better. After all, it is his story. It is his love letter to us. May we ever be captivated by him!

1. End-times prophecy

History has a way of repeating itself. Based on historical persecution of Christians and biblical prophecy of end times, there is an extremely high chance that there will come a day when our Bibles are taken away. You may think, "Even if they burn our Bibles, we will still have the Bible on the internet." No, my friend, the internet is the easiest place to delete information if the wrong person gains control of it. We are used to so much freedom as Americans, but we are living in the end times. We must prepare for persecution.

Jesus told us to be watchful for the end times. "Watch therefore, for you know neither the day nor the hour" (Matthew 25:13). But how can we be watchful if we do not know what to watch for? How can we keep from being deceived if we do not intimately know and understand the truth? How can that day not surprise us like a thief? (See Matthew 24:42-44; 1 Thessalonians 5:2-4.) We must know the truth. We must be keenly familiar with biblical prophecy. We are even to *encourage* one another with the words of prophecy about Jesus coming again (see 1 Thessalonians 4:18).

Consider memorizing some specific prophetic passages regarding the end times. These passages will help you discern the times we are currently in. They will be an ever-ready compass with which to align your heart, mind, and prayers in relation to current events. Man cannot steal or burn away that which is written on our hearts and minds.

A few prophetic passages for you to consider are listed in The Arsenal, section 9.

2. Favorite small book

What is your favorite small book of the Bible? Take the leap and commit it to memory. You will find such blessing in memorizing an entire book. We have been so blessed by having the entire book of James memorized. It was written as one letter, and memorizing it in its full context packs a greater punch than cherry-picking verses here and there. If you are having trouble picking a favorite small book, some of our recommendations are James, Philippians, Colossians, Ephesians, 2 Peter, 1 John, Jude, and Titus.

VICTORY STORY

Esther Eaton
College Student, Writer,
Former Piercing Word Intern

I first saw Piercing Word on a northeast tour stop in Maine, and it permanently changed my vision of God's Word. I had intellectually understood that the Bible was living and active, but never before had I understood the vitality, joy, complexity and power of Scripture. I memorized Philippians and that summer had a chance to perform it for a hundred girls at a summer camp. I'll never forget their excitement as the book came alive. They stood up applauding God's Word in its living beauty and power. Some expressed astonishment that Philippians was a "real letter" for "real people." Several of them even began memorizing Scripture together—an answer to prayer!

As an alternative to memorizing a small book of the Bible, you can choose to memorize a multi-chapter passage. Memorizing consecutive chapters in the Bible enables you to internalize longer stories or biblical sermons. Here are a couple recommended multi-chapter passages for you to consider.

Sermon on the Mount (Matthew 5–7). Memorizing the words of Jesus is like nothing else. It will change you profoundly. On the next page, be encouraged by Caleb Hughes' story of memorizing this precious passage.

John 14–17. This passage is also a three-chapter monologue by Jesus. These beautifully intimate chapters express Jesus's love for us, his unity with the Father, and our need to abide in him. It includes Jesus's prayer for us today.

3. Favorite large book
This is a really precious point in your memorization journey. When choosing a large book of the Bible to memorize, choose the one you are most passionate about.

Caleb Hughes

VICTORY STORY

Piercing Word Artistic Director,
Husband, Father

A few years ago, my wife and I were in a tight place financially. My wife had to step away from her job due to an unfortunate situation. And as a full-time seminary student who only worked part-time, I wasn't exactly flush with cash. Then we got the unexpected and wonderfully terrifying news—we were pregnant.

It was a mixed bag of emotions to say the least. While we were thankful for this new life, there were a lot of unknowns. I was only halfway through my degree, and we had no clear vision for where the Lord was leading us. While we were making friends, we lived across the country from family and our sense of community was still budding. And the financial questions of how to pay for school and a baby while still meeting our basic needs made the thought of raising a child even more daunting.

One night, we were sitting in bed and the financial stressors were especially intimidating. I remember holding my wife as she cried in my arms, and I silently asked God for words. He immediately reminded me of a passage that I had been memorizing. With tears running down our cheeks, I whispered:

> Therefore I tell you, do not be anxious about your life, what you will eat or what you will drink, nor about your body, what you will put on. Is not life more than food, and the body more than clothing? Look at the birds of the air: they neither sow nor reap nor gather into barns, and yet your heavenly Father feeds them. Are you not of more value than they? And which of you by being anxious can add a single hour to his span of life? And why are you anxious about clothing? Consider the lilies of the field, how they grow: they neither toil nor spin, yet I tell you, even Solomon in all his glory was not arrayed like one of

(continued)

these. But if God so clothes the grass of the field, which today is alive and tomorrow is thrown into the oven, will he not much more clothe you, O you of little faith? Therefore do not be anxious, saying, "What shall we eat?" or "What shall we drink?" or "What shall we wear?" For the Gentiles seek after all these things, and your heavenly Father knows that you need them all. But seek first the kingdom of God and his righteousness, and all these things will be added to you.

Therefore do not be anxious about tomorrow, for tomorrow will be anxious for itself. Sufficient for the day is its own trouble. (Matthew 6:25–34)

God used those words to bring divine comfort. They disarmed our fears and strengthened us for the journey, reminding us of God's steadfast love and faithful provision. Today, we are thankful for where God has brought us and how he perfectly orchestrated our steps in that season. Matthew 6 continues to be a passage that anchors our hearts and minds when the storms of uncertainty swirl around us. Praise God for his perfect Word.

However, if you are going to choose a large book to memorize, be sure that you have first memorized an entire chapter of the Bible, then memorized a small book of the Bible. Choose a large book of the Bible that is going to accomplish as many spiritual goals as possible.

One of our interns was considering memorizing a large book of the Bible and was trying to decide whether she should memorize Esther or Romans. Both are great books of the Bible. However, one is more multipurpose than the other from a spiritual perspective. You can determine the spiritual utility of a book of the Bible by simply going through the reasons why we should memorize God's Word that are listed in the first chapter of this book. As you do, ask yourself, "Are there verses or passages in this book of the Bible that will help me share my faith? fight temptation? know him? pray Scripture over others?" If you begin to answer these questions, you will quickly see that Romans has much more spiritually utility for daily living than Esther. Obviously, Esther is no less rich of a book of the Bible than Romans, and you should always follow what God is calling you to memorize even if it seems like a strange choice.

However, I encouraged our ambitious intern to choose Romans over Esther, especially as she was still new to memorizing large passages of Scripture. Later on, she could memorize Esther, and it could be a huge blessing to her. Likewise, you can prioritize your Bible memorization plans to accomplish the greatest spiritual good by simply asking yourself some of these simple questions. If we are going to spend the time to memorize an entire large book of the Bible, let's make it count for as much as we possibly can.

Challenges for Parents and Children

It has been said that children have never been good at obeying their parents, but they never cease to imitate them. So, the question I pose to you as a parent is this: how are you doing? If your child grew up and imitated exactly how you are living right now, would you be proud of him or her? What are the things you wish your child would do? Are *you* doing them?

Hopefully, one of the things we all desire for our children is that they know the Word of God. But they will have no desire for the Word if they do not see in us a desire for the Word. We need to set the example of memorizing God's Word ourselves. Parenthood is one of the busiest times with the least amount of time to yourself. How does one memorize in this beautiful, but crazy and chaotic season? Be sure to check out our section of On-the-Go Memorization Tactics for Life's Busy Seasons for some practical helps for Scripture memorization (Battle Resources: H).

SWORDPLAY TIP

Childhood is one of the best times to memorize Scripture.

Childhood is one of the best times to memorize. We often meet senior adults who express to us that they still remember Scriptures they

Glori Brubaker
VICTORY STORY
Mother of Five,
Piercing Word Board Member

Many verses are still hidden in my heart from my elementary school years. One teacher in particular assigned us a creative project: get in groups of four or five every single week and memorize a small chunk of Scripture. At the end of the week each group had to present their Scripture in the form of a skit, a song, rap, or any other creative idea we could find.

I am amazed at the lasting impression of those simple exercises. In fact, I still have many of those songs at the ready in my daily life as an adult.

memorized when they were children. Jesus said that, to enter the kingdom of heaven, we must become as a child (see Matthew 18:2–4). Jesus also prayed, "I thank you, Father, Lord of heaven and earth, that you have hidden these things from the wise and understanding and revealed them to little children" (Luke 10:21).

SWORDPLAY TIP

Do Bible memory with your children.

Children can start memorizing God's Word as young as two years of age. There are many short verses you could choose for your two year old to memorize; just make sure they are short, attainable, and easy to understand. Be sure to use hand motions, act them out, use lots of emotion and facial expressions, and involve excitement and energy. With all this, they will enjoy quoting their Bible verse with you every day.

As you memorize Scripture with your children, be sure to talk about what the verses mean and even do fun activities that illustrate the truth of the verse they just memorized.

In the next few sections, we give specific Scripture memorization challenges to implement as you are growing little people.

ABC Bible Verses

A fun way to start your kids on Bible memory is by teaching them a verse for every letter of the alphabet. You can find our ABC Bible Verses for Kids of All Ages in section I of The Arsenal. This set of twenty-six Bible verses includes life verses, gospel verses, temptation fighters, fear fighters, truths, and promises from God's Word. We have taken special care in selecting these ABC verses to ensure they are both spiritually nurturing and easy to remember. This is a great technique for both children and adults to memorize short, attainable verses, and the association with the English alphabet will jog your memory so you can consistently review what you have learned. Be sure to use hand motions or act the verses out, and use lots of emotion, facial expression, and energy. Your children will only be as excited about it as you are!

VICTORY STORY

Julia Hollinger
A Homeschool
Student

I had a fun experience memorizing Scripture with my sisters as a child. We were being homeschooled, and my mom decided we should memorize the Sermon on the Mount. For the first half of the year, we read it every day and recited it until we had it memorized. Then, in January, we started acting it out. For the first several days, we were just mapping out the different sections and assigning verses. Then came the fun part. We got to come up with creative ways to act it out.

My sisters and I had a lot of fun with it. We were allowed to be silly and funny, and acting it out made it much easier to remember. Of course, we had some hard days when we didn't want to work together and would get annoyed with each other, but in the end, I really enjoyed it. Acting out the verses brought them to life. I can still remember "chopping" my sister down as I recited, "Every tree that does not bear good fruit is cut down and thrown into the fire." Now, when I hear parts of the Sermon on the Mount, I can picture them in my head. It reminds me of the fun I had with my sisters as we memorized Scripture.

VICTORY STORY

Theresa Hollinger

Homeschooling Mother
of Five, Piercing Word Supporter

My favorite way to memorize Scripture is with my children. As a homeschooling mom, nothing brings me greater joy than the times I share with my children, learning and memorizing the Word of God. We start each morning with Bible class and follow with our memory work. At first, we would simply read the whole passage together each day and by the end of the year, the children would know it well.

However, several years ago, we took our memorization to a new, exciting level. I saw a Piercing Word presentation at our church and thought, "Wow, I could do this with my children!" We were memorizing Acts 7, which had a nice story-form flow to it. My oldest girls were in first and second grade at the time, and weren't quite ready for full-blown acting. So we made little puppets for each of the characters mentioned in Acts 7 as well as an Old Testament map of the areas mentioned. The girls took turns talking through the passage while moving the puppets along the map or making them talk to one another. This simple approach really helped the passage come to life!

The following year, we got ambitious and decided to tackle the Sermon on the Mount, which was much more than our standard forty verses. We spent the first half of the school year memorizing the verses. Then in January, my three oldest girls and I worked together to create a dramatic presentation of the Sermon on the Mount. The process wasn't always easy and there were plenty of tears and grumpy moments along the way. But I was so proud of their hard work, and honestly just as proud of my own perseverance to help them see it through to completion.

Over the years, we have continued to memorize Scripture together and create dramatic renditions, for example of David and Goliath. My younger son loved "killing" his older brother with his pantomime slingshot! As a homeschooling mom, I sometimes question whether I'm giving my children the optimal education I dreamed of for them. I know there are elements I've missed along the way, but the thing that brings me the most satisfaction and joy is knowing that I have been faithful in prioritizing our Bible times. In the scheme of life, there is nothing of greater value and importance for them to learn.

Be sure to do Bible memory *with* your children. It doesn't have to be just the kids memorizing Scripture or just you memorizing Scripture. This is a particularly great Scripture memory goal to start with if your kids are really little, but it is fun and upbuilding for all ages.

Memorizing Scripture songs

One of the best ways for kids (or anyone for that matter) to memorize Scripture is through song. We often have Scripture music playing in the background while our children play or while we eat a family meal. We especially love the *Hide 'Em in Your Heart* series by Steve Green. These songs are incredibly well done and are engaging for both kids and adults. We often center our family devotions around one of these Scripture songs. We dance around to the song as we sing along with it, and then afterward we read the same Bible verse aloud from the Bible and create hand motions that go along with it with our kids. Together, we talk in simple terms about what the verse means and how we can apply it practically to our lives.

We know of quite a few artists who have composed fun and engaging Scripture songs that kids love to learn. A list of these resources is provided in section 2 of The Arsenal.

Audio Bible verses

Listen to large chunks of audio Bible *with* your children to help with Pre-memorization and Review. We sometimes do this during meals or car rides with our kids. They *love* listening to the book of Jonah. If you do this consistently enough with an attainable chunk of Scripture, such as a single chapter, your kids will likely memorize it without even realizing they are doing it! You can even make a game of it to see who can quote along the most or who can beat the recorded voice by saying the upcoming verse before the recorded voice.

Teenager challenge

Consider assigning a chapter or a small book of the Bible for your teenager to memorize and recite before his or her high school graduation. We know a family that had each of their children memorize the book of James before they graduated from high school. What a beautiful and beneficial goal! If you homeschool, you can incorporate this as part of your children's Bible class.

Tag-teaming challenge for parents

Family challenges are wonderful, but it is still important and beneficial for Mom and Dad to have some alone time where they focus on active, personal memorization. Parents, you can work together to give each other ten to fifteen minutes each day or even two to three times a week to focus on doing some individual Active Memorization on your chosen Bible passages. We make time for what we deem important. Work together to make Scripture memory a reality for your family.

Pastor Challenges

Sermon-starter challenge

If you are a pastor of a local body of believers, consider looking ahead a couple of months on your preaching schedule and choose a chapter to memorize that would appropriately kick off one of your upcoming sermons. For those of you who preach on a verse or portion of a verse each Sunday, you can still memorize the entire chapter you are beginning or just completing. You could choose to simply quote the verse you are preaching on, but if you quote a longer portion of the passage, such as several consecutive verses or the entire chapter, your congregation will be far more encouraged to memorize the Word for themselves by watching and imitating your example.

As you prepare your sermon, memorize the chapter or passage you are using as a text. Then as you begin your message, quote the chapter with passion and vigor, as if you were speaking these words from the depths of your own soul. In order to successfully do this, you will first need to meditate on the Scripture and be sure you understand the heartbeat of the passage. Next, practice saying the passage in many different ways as you memorize it, so that when you share it with your congregation, you will be free to be naturally expressive and passionate. I also highly recommend rehearsing your passage aloud in the church sanctuary in front of an imaginary congregation, so you can get a feel for what it is like before your chosen Sunday rolls around.

When you first begin this, we encourage you to give yourself a couple of months to memorize and prepare. Then do it again before the end of the year. After that, you may begin to find a rhythm and set up a consistent schedule for memorizing certain sermon Scriptures throughout the year. Eventually, you may discover that you can actually memorize and quote all of the passages you are using in your sermon before you preach them. It is even possible to memorize and quote an entire chapter each week. How powerful to let God's Word speak first and speak for itself before you expound upon it!

Most chapters only take between one and five minutes to quote. Even the longest chapters are only about ten minutes in length. If you take the sermon-starter challenge, you will not regret it. You will benefit spiritually, and your people will be blessed and inspired to follow your example of knowing the Word.

On the next page you can read an exciting Victory Story of a pastor friend who took this challenge and how he and his congregation were immensely blessed.

Pastor sermon challenge
After you have memorized several chapters or passages to recite to your congregation as sermon starters, next memorize the Sermon on the Mount, Jesus's most famous sermon, found in Matthew chapters 5 to 7. Quote it to your congregation as your entire sermon. It is only fifteen minutes in length. Or you can take any one of the memorization challenges found in the Knowing Track and quote it as your entire sermon. This is a wonderful way to set the example. Remember, things are caught more than taught. If you set the example, people will begin to follow suit.

VICTORY STORY

Kent Rice

Husband, Pastor,
Community Leader

So it started with a friend of mine saying, "Kent, you have to check out this Piercing Word deal. They present the Bible word for word." So I did. I went to a Scripture performance. What I noticed right away is that I was receiving the Bible message differently. Aaron said that everybody can memorize a chapter, so I picked Romans 8, and thought, "My goal is to present this to my congregation." Of course, it was a joy to sit with the text because there's a crescendo in that chapter that you don't notice unless you are really, really studying it. As I was memorizing it, walking laps around the sanctuary, I got to one point and I just yelled, "Yes!" I smacked a big wooden beam so hard that my hand hurt for twenty minutes. It was beautiful. I presented the chapter to the congregation, and what I heard was the same thing that I felt when I saw it presented—which is that we received it differently.

Here's why I think that's important: I started playing guitar about thirty years ago. The first year I was very into it. But twenty-nine years later, I haven't improved at all because what I do every time is pick it up, play the same riffs, play the same little things and don't improve. So if we are interacting with the Bible the same way that we always have since childhood, there is not going to be a lot of revelation in that context.

If we can receive God's Word differently, then the Holy Spirit can step in and say, "You know what, I'm going to reveal something to you now in a way that's just between me and you that you can carry with you, not only to the end of your life, but into the next as well." Talk about something having impact! For me, if I can serve somebody with the Word in a way that replicates that and allows them to share it with somebody in that way, that's good stuff!

Marching Forward

Tackle your next project

No matter where you are in your memorization of God's Word right now, we encourage you to take your next step forward. Go beyond what you think is possible. If you haven't memorized anything yet, start with the Essentials Track. If you have memorized the Essentials Track, move on to the Growing Track. If you have done the Growing Track, tackle the Sharing Track and finally the Knowing Track.

Once you finish the various Bible Memorization Tracks in this book, our encouragement to you is to keep going. The spiritual discipline of Bible memorization is a life-long journey. Also, grab a friend or two to memorize with you and share the joy of memorizing Scripture with them.

> **SWORDPLAY TIP**
> The spiritual discipline of Scripture memorization is a lifelong journey. Take your next step forward.

No matter where you are in your journey, we would love to hear your Victory Story and how God has used memorizing Scripture to change your life and walk with Christ. You can share your story through the Contact Us form on our website: www.piercingword.org.

Going beyond

If you complete the various memorization challenges in this book, chances are you will officially be addicted to the Word, like me. At that point, you will probably start to have such crazy thoughts as "Maybe I will memorize the entire New Testament or better yet, the entire Bible." Or maybe you are not as crazy as me, and that idea sounds completely preposterous. Regardless of your position, I have a few thoughts I would like to share regarding my own endeavor to memorize the entire New Testament. It is humbling for me to admit that I did not finish this endeavor in the time frame I set out to do it in, nor have I finished it to this day . . . yet.

Although I grew a lot from the experience, it was the absolute hardest thing I have ever attempted to do. It came with many victories and high points, but also with many tears, long days, and some intense discouragement. In the second half of the endeavor, as it continued to drag into year two, the end crept further and further away, and my stamina waned. Many of the books I had memorized were falling into forgetfulness due to my own inability to do enough Maintenance Review to keep them. My wife walked with me through it all and she was *amazing*. I honestly think it would have driven me crazy had I attempted it while single.

Thanks to Emily, I have maintained my sanity to this day, and my experiences have driven me to ask the question, "What is truly most important to memorize and why?" Before I began memorizing the New Testament, in my own young and brash confidence, I probably would have written a book all about how you too can memorize the entire New Testament in a year. It is from all of these experiences that the Lord has shown me an enduring and truer perspective. With that perspective comes the understanding that, although God has blessed us with magnificent minds, we are also broken and fallen human beings, and we have imperfect and cursed brains that can forget things quickly. Until we have renewed bodies, we will struggle against this reality.

However, although it may be difficult for a single individual to memorize an entire testament or the entire Bible, it is possible for us to unite together as the church to memorize giant portions of Scripture collectively. I believe *this* is what God is calling the church of today to participate in. So get strapped in. Because you are about to be blown away with the possibilities of what God can do through a unified church that is truly seeking to know him better in the Church Challenges section of this chapter.

Church and Small Group Challenge

It is easy to think of Scripture memorization as being mainly for personal growth. We want to gently tuck our fingers under your chin and lift your eyes from the path up to the horizon. Memorizing God's Word is part of a much bigger vision than each person personally falling in love with God through his Word. When we collectively pursue knowing God through his Word and tuck his truth deep into our hearts, *that* is when revival happens. That is when the church begins to operate as it should.

So often, we find our churches bound by the lies of the culture around us, conforming to the standards of this world rather than being transformed by Christ and the renewal of our minds. When the body of Christ collectively knows the truth and is set free from the lies of the culture, then the gospel will reach the ends of the earth in no time and Jesus will return. That is when the church can finally be unified as Jesus prayed that we would be:

> SWORDPLAY TIP
>
> **Unite together as the church to memorize giant portions of Scripture collectively.**

> I do not ask for these only, but also for those who will believe in me through their word, that they may all be one, just as you, Father, are in me, and I in you, that they also may be in us, so that the world may believe that you have sent me. The glory that you have given me I have given to them, that they may be one even as we are one, I in them and you in me, that they may become perfectly one, so that the world may know that you sent me and loved them even as you loved me. (John 17:20–23)

The verse says, "that they may become perfectly one, so that the world may know that you sent me." Our unity as the body of Christ will speak to the world the truth about the lordship of Jesus. How can we be unified as the church unless we rally around the center of our beliefs, the Bible?

Memorizing Scripture together as a church body can change how we collectively think and function. As each person allows himself to be changed by the truth from the inside out, that church body will be more effective for the kingdom of God. We believe that when we know God's Word as a church, true discipleship and evangelism will happen organically.

> SWORDPLAY TIP
>
> **Memorizing Scripture together as a church body can change how we collectively think and function.**

What if every church body committed to memorizing entire books of the Bible collectively? What if every Christian chose to memorize a verse, a chapter, a book, or some large chunk of Scripture? Some large churches would be able to collectively memorize an entire Testament or even the entire Bible in only a few weeks if the specific Bible passages were properly organized and assigned. Just think of it!

The Church and Small Group Challenge is perhaps the most exciting challenge in this book to us. It calls us as believers to unite together in knowing God's Word. We challenge you and your church or small group to commit to collectively memorize an entire book of the Bible as you study it together. The amazing thing is, it's probably a lot more attainable than it sounds. For instance, did you know that a group of fifty people can memorize the entire book of Philippians collectively if each person memorizes only two or three verses? In fact, we have included a Church Challenge Chart in section 11 of The Arsenal to help you discover exactly what memorizing an entire book of the Bible could mean for your group. We have outlined for you how many verses each person in your small group or church would need to memorize in order to accomplish each goal.

The Church Challenge Chart is a helpful tool for engaging every member of your small group or church in memorizing God's Word in a fun and unifying manner. More specifically, this chart helps determine what books of the Bible your church or small group could collectively memorize if every person in your group memorized only one or two verses. Before you look at the chart, be sure to consider the following:

1. Figure out approximately how many people are in your small group or church (ten people? a hundred people? a thousand people?).

2. Find out if there is a book of the Bible you are already studying or preaching through this year or next year that would be a natural fit for your small group or church to memorize.

3. If this is your group's first time taking this challenge, be sure to choose a smaller verse number assignment for each participant; for example, one verse per person, rather than ten verses per person.

4. Consider choosing a New Testament book, Psalms, or Proverbs over a random Old Testament book. The reason I suggest this is not to belittle the Old Testament. I *love* the Old Testament, and I believe we should read and study it more than most of us do currently. The Old Testament passages are hugely important to understanding God's whole counsel. However, if each person is only assigned one to five verses to memorize from a book of the Bible, we want to ensure everyone has a good experience. The New Testament books, Psalms, and Proverbs avoid having people assigned to what seem to be less encouraging and less immediately applicable passages, such as genealogies, Levitical instructions, or curses upon people groups. Don't get me wrong; these passages have enormous value but can be difficult to apply when confined to small segments that are memorized out of context.

Of course, in order to be successful at this group Bible memorization endeavor, you will have to create a plan with a deadline (such as a Scripture Sharing Celebration or a filming), assign or encourage accountability partners, and provide a basic schedule. Corporate accountability will be the biggest driving force in your plan, which will help people get to the finish line of memorization. This level of accountability is best exercised by the group collectively sharing the book of the Bible in a predetermined format as an encouragement to the entire group. You can share your book of the Bible in one of several ways:

1. One of the easiest ways to do this in our high-tech culture is to ask the participants in your group to make a video of themselves quoting their passage, as a selfie or with their accountability partner. Then have them submit their videos by a certain date to someone in your group who can put these videos together and underlay it with instrumental music. You can then share this video in a church service as a celebration of what you have done together.

2. Another strategy to celebrate and share the verses you have memorized is have a day assigned for a more professional filming of each person's verse. Each person signs up for a time slot to quote their passage in front of the camera. (Be sure to

have them quote their verses two or three times for the camera. It is a good idea to tell them to do a practice run while filming it, and then keep filming while they do it for real.) Then have someone on your staff edit the video together, adding some instrumental music underneath it. As suggested above, you can then share this video in a church service as a celebration of what you have done together!

3. Another option is to hold a Scripture Sharing Celebration of the entire book, which is similar to a recital or a Scriptorium by our friends at Scripture Memory Fellowship. This could be done as a part of your regular meeting or be a separate celebratory event. Before everyone arrives, print (or write) the verse references on paper that is set on or taped to each person's seat. Tell everyone find their assigned verse reference and sit in the appropriate chair. Then the first person proceed to the microphone at the front of the room to share their verse(s) for the group. The second and third persons go to the microphone at the same time as the first and wait to the side of the microphone. As soon as the first person shares their verse(s), the second steps to the microphone, and the fourth person walks to the front of the room. This continues in similar fashion until the entire book of the Bible has been shared.

The key to success for any of these celebrations lies in encouraging all participants to share their passage with the emotion, enthusiasm, and intention with which the passage was written. No one wants to listen to a hundred people read Scripture in monotone. However, everyone will be riveted and enthralled by watching one hundred people truly enjoying God's Word and sharing it with their whole selves.

As you consider what book of the Bible your group should choose to memorize, check out the Church Challenge Chart in section 11 of The Arsenal at the back of this book and choose your book of the Bible to memorize as a group. If your church or group is large enough, you may even consider tackling an entire Testament together. For instance, a group of one thousand people could all memorize a verse a day for one week and together collectively memorize the entire New Testament. With unity in the Body of Christ, the possibilities are astounding.

Let's lift up our eyes. Memorizing Scripture is all about deepening our own personal walk with the Lord, about falling more in love with him and knowing him more profoundly. But it goes beyond our individual selves. Each of us is but a tiny member of the entire body of Christ and *how we personally function affects how the body functions as a whole.* We invite you to dream of what your church could accomplish together in unity, as together you memorize the Word of God.

1. Now it's time to dream big and think about your long-term Bible memorization journey by filling out your Bible Memorization Marching Orders in section A of Battle Resources. In this Marching Orders worksheet, you can write your life verse, your chosen gospel verses, and your temptation fighters and fear fighters. You can also write your desired Growth Track passages, Sharing Track passages, and Knowing Track passages. Use this time to prayerfully navigate and create your personalized Bible Memorization Marching Orders based on the suggestions in this chapter and the resources in The Arsenal Sections B through J.

2. Take a look at the ABC Bible Verses for Kids of All Ages and consider using this as part of your Essentials Track or as a family Bible memorization guide.

3. Choose a Bible passage from your Marching Orders worksheet to start memorizing right now. Write your chosen passage at the top of your Plan of Attack in section B of Battle Resources.

4. Log in to the Warriors of the Word Facebook Group and share a picture of your chosen passage, why you picked it, and how you are hoping it will impact your life. If you don't have Facebook, tell someone in your life this week what Bible passage you are memorizing, why you picked it, and how you are hoping it will impact your life.

5. Write several Scripture passages or books of the Bible that your church or small group could memorize collectively based on the Church Challenge Chart in section 11 of The Arsenal.

CHAPTER 4

Formulating Your Plan of Attack

The heart of man plans his way, but the Lord establishes his steps.
~ Proverbs 16:9

"Emily! Guess what? I just figured out that it is possible to memorize the entire New Testament in one year if one memorizes at a rate of twenty-two new verses every day!" My bride-to-be met my excitement with genuine curiosity, which is a testament to my wife's unshakable love for me even while we were engaged. "Do you really think it's possible to do that?" she said. "I don't know," I replied. "But I really want to try. Up to this point, the most verses I have memorized in a single day is about twelve. But if twelve is possible in a day, then twenty-two is definitely possible with a little more time."

About six months later, after our marriage ceremony and several months of planning, I was well into the project. We called it "Aaron Is Memorizing the New Testament" or AIMTNT. After a month of memorizing, I realized I needed a day off each week to catch my breath or to use as a catch-up day. So I swallowed hard and made the decision to switch to memorizing thirty new verses every day, six days a week. This required approximately two hours a day of memorization and review, which was, quite frankly, an exhausting pace. Just in case you are curious, this is *not* a pace we recommend imitating.

AARON

In the same manner, just as my project of memorizing the New Testament required intentional planning and accountability, your Bible memorization projects will likewise need proper planning to be successful.

Even though one of the main goals of this book is to show you that memorization can truly be a fun, memorable, and even exciting experience, we would be lying to tell you that memorization is all fun and games. Memorization is also *work*, which is *not a bad thing.* The ability to work hard toward a goal is a beautiful gift and can even be a fun and rewarding experience. Now we will share how to incorporate the necessary disciplines into this art of memorization so that you can have an encouraging and successful experience.

Where to Memorize

EMILY

First, let's talk about a common misconception. Many people believe that you can memorize anywhere you want. The truth is that you can *review* anywhere you want, but Active Memorization requires *a focused time and place with limited distractions.* Memorize in a place where you feel alone. For better or for worse, we are generally self-conscious as humans. In order to feel completely free to be creative with the learning style techniques discussed in this book, you will need privacy. It is also helpful to pick a place with limited distractions. You may feel alone in your bedroom, but your bedroom often holds too many distractions: your smartphone beeping at you, unfinished books, clothes that need to be organized, laundry to be put away, a bed that is begging you to curl up and take a nap—you get the idea. If the room you selected is a place where you feel alone but is full of distractions, try picking someplace else. Some of our favorite places to memorize are a quiet corner outside in God's creation, a finished basement, or a guest room. Outside tends to be rejuvenating and inspiring. A finished basement or guest room often holds fewer personal things to distract you.

> **SWORDPLAY TIP**
>
> **Active Memorization requires a focused time and place where you feel alone and have limited distractions.**

When to Memorize

Once again, a common memorization misconception is that anyone can memorize at any time. This is only partly true. You can technically memorize at any given time, but some times will be more efficient. We all have certain times of the day (or night) where we feel most energetic and alert. These are the ideal times to memorize. This is not to say that we should never attempt Scripture memorization when we are tired and grumpy. In fact, Scripture could help turn a sour perspective around. However, we want to feel encouraged and successful by our memorization times, so it is wise to plan to do memorization, as much as possible, during times when we are likely to feel energetic and alert. By all means, use sleepless nights and hard emotional days or moments to spontaneously run to Scripture and memorize God's Word. But as a norm, plan your intentional memorization times during your favorite portion of the day.

Making a Memorization Plan

If you fail to plan, you plan to fail. It sounds a bit harsh, but there is so much truth in this statement. If you want to succeed at memorization, you must make a plan. This is simpler than it sounds. After you decide *what* you are going to memorize, *where* you are going to memorize, and *when* you are going to memorize, half of your memorization plan is already in place. Now you need to decide how many verses a day (or week) you will memorize. It is often difficult for people to know how to decide what their pace should be, so here is a general idea:

Beginner: one verse per week or one verse every other day (one to four verses a week)

Early Intermediate: one to two verses a day (five to ten verses a week)

Intermediate: three to four verses a day (fifteen to twenty verses a week)

Advanced: five or more verses a day (twenty-five or more verses a week)

These pace recommendations are only referring to the Active Memorization stage. Obviously, if you are doing Active Memorization on a verse each day, you will have to do some Pre-memorization in the days leading up to that day and review in the days following that day. So not all of the work for that one verse is happening in one day. But you should only need one day of what we call Active Memorization on any given verse if you successfully do your Pre-memorization and review work in the days surrounding it. In fact, once you get to the Growth Track and the Knowing Track, we do not recommend memorizing a passage, chapter, or book of the Bible at any rate slower than one verse per day. If you do, you are likely to lose momentum and never finish.

A quick disclaimer about the advanced memorization pace—this is usually a short term memorization sprint, not something that is done every day for years at a time. No matter what category you are in, though, it is important to have a specific deadline for finishing your passage.

When you are done with that one, begin another passage with a fresh deadline. This will keep you feeling successful and allow for the sometimes necessary breaks from Bible memorization in different circumstances. After you decide how many verses a day you will do, calculate how many days it will take you to finish memorizing your selected Scripture. We recommend memorizing five or six days a week instead of seven; this allows you to have a day or two off, which can be helpful for playing catch-up if you happened to miss a day that week. Or it might give you time to focus on review. Use the Plan of Attack in the Battle Resources section B of this book as you begin to make your own Bible memorization plan. Feel free to make copies and fill it out so you have something tangible and specific to reference. This Plan of Attack worksheet will lead you through the steps you need to take to make a successful Bible memorization plan.

Memorization Definitions

Many people approach memorization without any plan or idea of how they are going to get from point A (information on a page) to point B (information stored in their brain). They simply pound, pound, pound the information by either reading or repeating the words over and over in the hope that somehow the information will eventually stick. I also tried this haphazard approach during my homeschool years as a child with spotty success. Sometimes I understood why it didn't work, but sometimes I did not.

If you can grasp the simple yet profound steps of the Piercing Word Bible Memorization Process and put them into practice, then you will find memorization is attainable for you. What once was a dark and untraveled path will be well-lit and marked with familiar landmarks that help guide your course along the journey. We will start with a few definitions. You encountered these in the Boot Camp Packing List. They are included here as a review.

Pre-memorization—This is time spent reading, listening to, or studying the text with the purpose of truly understanding it. The goal of this time is to understand, not to memorize. However, the understanding gained in this phase is essential before moving into the Active Memorization phase.

Active Memorization—This is a one-time memorization experience with a specific and attainable goal and set time frame. You are alone, with limited distractions, using 100 percent of your focus and attention on memorization.

Solidification Review—This happens every day for at least a week after actively memorizing a verse or a passage. It can be done by oneself or with a friend, but still requires all of your focus and attention.

Maintenance Review—This happens once a week or once a month for an indefinite period of time or until you move on to another passage. It can be done while multitasking.

Re-memorization—This is only necessary when you have waited too long to review a passage that was previously memorized. Although this can be done twice as fast as regular Active Memorization, it requires the same diligence and focus.

All of these steps can layer on top of each other in order to help you have a seamless Bible memorization experience. Understanding the different aspects of memorization will help you differentiate your purposes for each moment you spend on a given passage. For instance, if you are memorizing a chapter that is thirty verses long, your approach could look something like the chart on the next page. This example memorization plan is also included in section D of Battle Resources. You can create your own plan just like this by using the Personal Memorization Plan Calculator Tool, which you can download at warriorsofthewordbook.org/resources.

Example Memorization Plan

For memorizing one chapter (thirty verses) at a rate of one verse per day

	Pre-Memorization
DAY 1	✔ Read the entire chapter ✔ Read the chapters before and after it ✔ Read some background on the who, what, when, where, why, and how of this passage
DAY 2	✔ Read the chosen chapter once ✔ Look up any unfamiliar words ✔ Read any commentary on the passage as needed ✔ Paraphrase the chapter in your own words

	ACTIVE MEMORIZATION	SOLIDIFICATION REVIEW	MAINTENANCE REVIEW
DAY 3	Verse 1		
DAY 4	Verse 2	Verse 1	
DAY 5	Verse 3	Verses 1-2	
DAY 6	Verse 4	Verses 1-3	
DAY 7	Verse 5	Verses 1-4	
DAY 8	Verse 6	Verses 1-5	
DAY 9	Verse 7	Verses 1-6	
DAY 10	Verse 8	Verses 1-7	
DAY 11	Verse 9	Verses 2-8	
DAY 12	Verse 10	Verses 3-9	
DAY 13	Verse 11	Verses 4-10	
DAY 14	Verse 12	Verses 5-11	
DAY 15	Verse 13	Verses 6-12	
DAY 16	Verse 14	Verses 7-13	Verses 1-6
DAY 17	Verse 15	Verses 8-14	
DAY 18	Verse 16	Verses 9-15	
DAY 19	Verse 17	Verses 10-16	
DAY 20	Verse 18	Verses 11-17	
DAY 21	Verse 19	Verses 12-18	
DAY 22	Verse 20	Verses 13-19	
DAY 23	Verse 21	Verses 14-20	Verses 1-13
DAY 24	Verse 22	Verses 15-21	
DAY 25	Verse 23	Verses 16-22	
DAY 26	Verse 24	Verses 17-23	
DAY 27	Verse 25	Verses 18-24	
DAY 28	Verse 26	Verses 19-25	
DAY 29	Verse 27	Verses 20-26	
DAY 30	Verse 28	Verses 21-27	Verses 1-20
DAY 31	Verse 29	Verses 22-28	
DAY 32	Verse 30	Verses 23-29	
DAY 33		Verses 24-30	Verses 1-30
DAY 34		Verses 25-30	Verses 1-30
DAY 35		Verses 26-30	Verses 1-30
DAY 36		Verses 27-30	Verses 1-30
DAY 37		Verses 28-30	Verses 1-30

In this kind of memorization plan, you can randomly decide to include Maintenance Review of past verses whenever you wish. This is a basic guideline. And honestly, the Maintenance Review is where the real blessing takes effect. Make sure you begin using it as soon and as often as you can.

We highly recommend that you start each memorization time with Active Memorization and then move on to Solidification Review and then to

SWORDPLAY TIP

Begin each memorization time with Active Memorization before moving on to review. This will ensure your best energies go toward the hardest task.

Maintenance Review. If you do it the other way around, you will use your best energies on polishing the old verses and never be able to move on to the new verses. It may seem counterintuitive to do it like this, but if you trust the process and you are consistent in doing your Solidification Review each day, you will have no trouble maintaining the passages you actively memorize. Also, you will give your Active Memorization your best foot forward every day.

Remember, you want to give 100 percent of your attention, focus, and energy during Active Memorization. If you do this, your Solidification Review will be much easier.

Another note: if you are free spirited in nature, you might feel stressed out just by looking at this kind of plan. Not to worry, your plan can look different and can be more creative and flexible—but you still need a plan. Your plan still needs to include all the phases of memorization and must be implemented consistently to have the desired results.

SWORDPLAY TIP

Give all your attention, focus, and energy during Active Memorization.

Consistency is key. If you fail to do your Solidification Review for several days in a row, you will end up having to re-memorize passages, which is ultimately more time-consuming and often disheartening.

Brad Myer

VICTORY STORY

Actor, Student, Piercing Word Team
Member/Former Intern

When creating your memorization schedule, don't feel
pressured to make it super-regimented. Do what works best for
you. Some people find it easier to have a set amount of time
each day or each week that they work on memorization, say,
one hour a day. Some people have a goal of a certain number
of verses to memorize each day or week, say, ten verses a
week. This gives a little more flexibility.

I memorize by paragraph. When I start a memorization
session, I will have a goal of memorizing a paragraph chunk
or two, and I will spend as much time as it takes to get through
it. In a lot of books, the passages are broken up into similar
paragraph lengths. One chunk may be ten verses, the next
nine, and the next thirteen. I find this method works for me
because it doesn't allow me to limit myself by saying, "I'll only
memorize ten verses today," or "I'm only spending twenty
minutes on this today." It also helps me process the passage
and understand it better.

All in all, do what works for you! If you find having a regimented
schedule is best for you, then great! Go for it. But if that type
of regiment seems daunting, know that it is okay to be flexible
with how much you memorize and when you do it.

Above is a personal example of a less structured approach to making
a plan for memorizing a large portion, chapter, or book of the Bible.

The Importance of Accountability

Imagine it's New Year's Eve and you are making New Year's
resolutions with your friends. Your New Year's resolution is to get
in shape by going to the gym to work out every day in the coming
year, but you are the only one with that goal in your group of friends.
So the next day, you head to the local gym and sign up for a gym

membership. Then you begin to get up an hour earlier every morning to head to the gym. How long do you think that New Year's resolution will last? A week or two? A month, maybe?

Now imagine yourself back at that same New Year's Eve party a year later. You resolve again to get in shape. This time, one of your close friends makes the same resolution. The next day you head to the gym together to renew your memberships. You both agree to get up an hour earlier than normal three days a week and meet each other at the gym to work out. How long do you think that workout plan is going to last? Two to three months? A full year, maybe? You see, accountability takes us further than we would be able to go on our own.

We often will not do something for ourselves but will do it if we know someone else is counting on us or if someone else's needs or goals are at stake. Accountability channels the "power of the other," as Henry Cloud illuminates dynamically in his book entitled *The Power of the Other*.[4] Having another human being expectantly cheering us on is an extremely powerful motivator that creates strength within us that didn't exist before.

The dictionary definition of "accountable" is "(of a person, organization or institution): required or expected to justify actions or decisions; responsible; subject to give an account; answerable."[5] This is not something that is talked about much in our society. Accountability with another mature, godly believer is of utmost value. When we know that someone is going to check up on us and ask us about our movement toward a specific goal, we are suddenly motivated. We want to save face; we want to impress; we want to feel successful; we want others to be proud of us. These are all natural inclinations, so let's use these natural bents to our advantage.

> **SWORDPLAY TIP**
>
> **Accountability takes us further than we would be able to go on our own.**

Find someone who will be willing to consistently ask for a report on how your Scripture memory is going. If possible, find someone else who also desires to memorize a passage of Scripture and check in with each other in person or over

EMILY

the phone at least once a week. Quote to each other whatever you have memorized so far. Accountability is helpful because not only can you hold each other to your set goals but you can pray for and encourage each other on the difficult days.

The Power of Deadlines

Deadlines are another form of accountability. I have always been a dreamer and struggle with being easily distracted. Deadlines have frequently been a strong motivating force. I can't remember ever having a consistent exercise regimen until I attended Elim Bible Institute, where the school required a certain amount of time spent in physical exercise each week. It was then that I fell in love with regularly going on walks outdoors. The tiny little town had only one stoplight in the center of town. Even so, I loved strolling its quaint vintage streets, exploring the antique shops and hunting for parks or fields where I could get away and have time with Jesus and my journal.

For as long as I can remember, my vivid imagination has been spinning fiction stories. But as I have tried to birth those stories through my pen or keypad, a growing percentage of my tales languished unfinished, deserted for the next new plot that had sprouted in my mind. When I decided to take an online writer's course where a published author mentored me and assigned specific story goals and deadlines, suddenly my collection of finished stories bulked up because I had built-in accountability, deadlines, and the ensuing reward or punishment of good or bad grades. All this provided sufficient motivation to drive me to the task of completion.

I know that I am not alone in this; it is true for many people. Because of this, we strongly encourage you to schedule a Scripture Sharing Celebration before you begin memorizing. This could mean quoting your memorized passage to a friend, your small group, your whole church, or at a family gathering. You could recite it to your youth group, your Bible study group, or maybe even your coworkers. This is going to sound intimidating to some, but remember, this is not a performance unless you want it to be. It is simply a scheduled time for you to share your passage with others. The goal is to be genuine and expressive with the memorized text, but there is no acting required. We recommend scheduling your Scripture Sharing Celebration for two weeks after you are supposed to be finished memorizing. This allows you a week to play catch-up if necessary and another week to solidify and practice reciting it before you are in front of an audience.

The point of scheduling a Scripture Sharing Celebration is not just for accountability; it is also to encourage your

SWORDPLAY TIP

Schedule a Scripture Sharing Celebration before you begin memorizing.

fellow brothers and sisters in Christ. When memorizing Scripture, especially large portions or books of the Bible, there is often an innate fear that sharing it in front of other people is prideful and should be avoided. What a lie of the enemy this is! This fear of pride makes us selfishly hoard a blessing that we could be showering upon everyone in our path. Let me encourage you with the words of James:

> Who is wise and understanding among you? By his good conduct *let him show his works in the meekness of wisdom.* But if you have bitter jealousy and selfish ambition in your hearts, *do not boast* and be false to the truth. This is not the wisdom that comes down from above, but is earthly, unspiritual, demonic. For where jealousy and selfish ambition exist, there will be disorder and every vile practice. But the wisdom from above is first pure, then peaceable, gentle, open to reason, full of mercy and good fruits, impartial and sincere. And a harvest of righteousness is sown in peace by those who make peace. (James 3:13–18, emphasis added)

Although it is possible to share memorized Scripture with a prideful and boastful spirit, it is equally possible to share it with a meek and humble spirit and sow a harvest of righteousness. Let us follow the advice and admonition of James and let our light shine before others, that they may see our good works and give glory to our Father in Heaven (see Matthew 5:16).

It's not about us receiving glory, but it is all about God receiving glory when we share the Scripture we have memorized. When we share our passage in front of others, we can ensure God gets the glory by sharing how God has used that Scripture passage in our own heart and life. He is glorified when we give him the glory and praise for his work in our lives.

SWORDPLAY TIP

Memorizing and reciting Scripture is all about God receiving glory not us.

There is a special blessing in hearing God's spoken Word. Let's give our pride and our fear of what others think of us over to the Lord, and let's share this precious gift of memorized Scripture with our Christian family. Satan is trying to keep us fearful, independent, and silent. But we can courageously move beyond our fears and speak out the Word to others. Let's live in community and think of others first. You never know: sharing one memorized passage of Scripture could spark an entire movement in your church to memorize the Word of God.

Creating a Memorization Journal

After you have made a memorization plan and budgeted your time, consider getting a journal in which to record your progress each day. Aaron did this when he was memorizing the New Testament. He has an entire journal that gives a day-by-day, blow-by-blow account of every memorization and review session he had for the entire year and a half.

Creating a journal like this is not a necessity, but it is extremely helpful if you want to improve your memorization skill by tangibly assessing your progress and learning from your own mistakes. It was especially key for Aaron in learning how he worked best. He would record the number of verses he successfully memorized that day (as opposed to the planned or attempted number of verses) as well as the specific passages he reviewed. He would also record the time of day, the location where he memorized, whether it came easily or came with much difficulty (and why, if he knew), and other notes about the atmosphere, distractions, obstacles, problems, physicality, or attitudes that affected his memorization and review sessions.

We believe you will find a memorization journal to be a helpful tool as you seek to grow in your personal memorization abilities.

From Plans to Lifestyle

As you begin to use these strategies to create your Plan of Attack, please know that not everything we have memorized was because we planned it out. Once memorizing Scripture becomes a spiritual discipline and a spiritual tool that you are comfortable with, you can memorize Scripture at almost any time. For example, you might be reading a chapter of Scripture and find a verse through which God speaks to you, then memorize it before you finish your time in the Word that day. We have often done this. In so doing, you can more easily and readily recall what you have read earlier that day and take the essential truth with you as you go.

Everyone's memorization plan is going to be somewhat different. The key is keeping the essential elements intact, while making it your own and having fun with it. In fact, there are probably some creative strategies not mentioned in this book that could work for you. We have done our best to compile the most widely used and effective tactics we are aware of, but also realize that we neither know everything nor have been everywhere. The key is to ensure you are incorporating the essentials of the Piercing Word Bible Memorization Process.

Your progress through the memorization process

- ☑ Know Why
- <u>Know How</u>
- ☑ **PLAN IT**
- ☐ Understand It
- ☐ See It, Say It, Do It
- ☐ Review It
- ☐ Apply It
- (Repeat)

1. Fill out the Quick Start Battle Plan on the next page as well as the "Plan It" section of your Plan of Attack in section B of Battle Resources. The Quick Start Battle Plan enables you to have your current Bible Memorization Plan at a glance for your own reference as well as for your accountability partner. The "Plan It" section of the Plan of Attack will help you think through your plan strategically and can be used to educate your Quick Start Battle Plan.

2. Share your Quick Start Battle Plan with your accountability partner and log in to the Warriors of the Word Facebook Group and share it with the group. You can either take photos of your written answers in the Quick Start Battle Plan and post them or type your answers in a post.

   For Example: *"Hi Warrior friends! I just filled out the Quick Start Battle Plan, and I wanted to share it with you all.*

   Chosen Passage: *Romans 8*

   Accountability Partner: *Taylor Martin*

   Weekly Accountability Check-in Time: *Every Wednesday at 8pm (in person or phone call depending on the week)*

   Memorization Deadline: *September 25*

   Weekly and Daily Memorization Goals: *It has thirty-nine verses, so I am going to memorize three verses a day, five days a week. I am going to memorize each weekday and leave the weekends as review/catch-up days.*

   Location and Time of Day to Memorize: *In the field behind our office building, from 12:30-1:00 pm each day on my lunch break. On weekends, I will review in our backyard at 8 pm for fifteen minutes after getting the kids in bed.*

   Scripture Sharing Celebration: *I am going to recite Romans 8 for my church small group on September 10. I have already checked with my small group leader and scheduled it and they are really excited! I am nervous, but excited as well!*

Quick Start Battle Plan

Chosen Passage: _____

Accountability Partner:_____

Weekly Accountability Check-in Time and Communication Method:

_____

_____

_____

_____

_____

Memorization Deadline:_____

Weekly and Daily Memorization Goals:_____

_____

_____

_____

_____

_____

_____

_____

Location(s) and Time(s) of Day to Memorize and Review:

_____

_____

_____

_____

Scripture Sharing Celebration Date, Time, and Location:

_____

_____

CHAPTER 5

Become Acquainted With Your Weapons

Understanding Your Passage

There are some things in them that are hard to understand,
which the ignorant and unstable twist to their own destruction,
as they do the other Scriptures. ~ 2 Peter 3:16

"For this Melchizedek, king of Salem . . . umm . . . priest of the Most High God, met Abraham returning from the . . . the slaughter of the kings and . . . and . . . ugh!"

I was pacing back and forth in our small bedroom, attempting to memorize large portions of the book of Hebrews. I had dived right in and tried to hammer the passages into my brain but found that they simply refused to stick in my memory. Frustrated, I retreated from the room to lament to my husband.

"Aaron!" I complained. "Hebrews is *so hard* to memorize! I've tried and tried, but it just won't stick in my brain."

Aaron frowned thoughtfully. "Are you sure you understand what the passage is saying?"

With that one question, the truth dawned on me. Riddled with ancient biblical traditions and complex spiritual pictures, the passage didn't make sense to my twenty-first-century mind. I had to admit I did

EMILY

not fully understand the passage. Therefore, my brain felt it had nothing logical to grasp on to and store in its memory bank. Aaron and I sunk down together onto our chocolate-colored pleather couch and cracked open the beloved book. We intentionally studied the passages, flipping back pages to Old Testament references and hashing out old Hebrew customs and the spiritual pictures the author of Hebrews was painting. Then, when I felt I had begun to grasp the meaning of the passages, I headed back into my "memorizing room" to start afresh.

"For this Melchizedek [I bounced my right pointer finger through the air to loosely imitate a walking man] king of Salem [I placed an invisible crown on my head], priest of the Most High God [I mimicked holding a bowl of atonement full of blood from the sacrifice] met Abraham returning [my left pointer finger bounced through the air to "meet" the finger from my right hand] from the slaughter of the kings [I drew a finger across my neck to symbolize slaughter] and to him Abraham apportioned a tenth part of everything" [I pretended to receive an offering plate and put an invisible pinch of money into it to symbolize the tithing happening in the passage].

> **SWORDPLAY TIP**
>
> You cannot memorize something you do not understand.

Suddenly, the words and concepts began to stick. I now could picture what was happening in my mind's eye. Because I now understood the passage, I was able to create motions to portray the meaning. The hand motions I added also helped to create a memorable physical picture for my eyes and body to latch on to and helped trigger the words of the passage in my brain anytime I was tempted to draw a blank. I was elated about my sudden success and determined to share my discovery with others, so they didn't make the same mistake I did.

Pre-memorization

Pre-memorization is spending time reading, listening to, or studying the text with the purpose of truly understanding it. The goal of this time is to understand, not to memorize. However, the understanding gained in this phase is essential before moving into the Active Memorization phase. Each person will require a different amount of pre-memorization for each piece of text. In fact, the pre-memorization phase could range from simply reading the passage a couple of times to spending days, weeks, or even months in deep exegetical research. If it is an easy-to-understand or familiar passage, you may find that all you need is to read it or listen to it a few times in order to gain an adequate understanding of the passage before moving on to the Active Memorization Phase.

However, sometimes we may be so familiar with a passage, that we think we understand it when we really do not. We have a friend who has a great way to ensure she truly understands the text before memorizing it. After she reads the passage a couple of times, she paraphrases it in her own words. If she is able to say the passage in her own words and feels that she successfully captured the essence of what that passage is about in her paraphrased version, then she knows she can move on to Active Memorization. We highly recommend incorporating this practice into your memorization process.

If you come to a verse or passage that you do not fully understand, *do not move on to active memorization* until you have sought out further explanation.

If you go on to Active Memorization before truly understanding the passage, it will feel more like memorizing numbers in a line (which is very possible, but seemingly difficult at first glance, and it requires a different memorization technique than is taught in this book). It is very difficult to memorize something you do not understand. Your brain has no reason to remember it if it does not make sense to you. It cannot be properly processed and filed into the brain's categorical storage system.

Pray and ask God to reveal to you the truth of the passage so you can understand it.

SWORDPLAY TIP

Recommended Pre-Memorization Protocol

1. Pray and ask God to reveal to you the truth of the passage in a way that you can understand. He loves to answer this prayer because he wants us to know him intimately.

2. Read the passage out loud a couple times and then see if you can paraphrase the passage in your own words.

3. Ask yourself, "Do I know the Who, What, When, Where, Why, and How of this passage?" Then look up the context in which the passage was written. Who wrote it and to whom did they write it? When and where was it written? What was the initial reason for the writing?

4. If you have a Study Bible, read the notes found at the bottom of the page about that passage. It may also be helpful to look at the notes at the very beginning of that book of the Bible that may give more information about the author and the historical context. (The ESV Study Bible by Crossway is an excellent resource for this type of research)

5. Look up commentary on the passage or ask a pastor, teacher, parent, or friend who is mature in their faith and walk with God how they read and understand the passage.

6. Look up the definitions of any unfamiliar words in the Dictionary.

7. If you want to go even deeper, research the Greek and Hebrew meaning of key words in the passage using a Strong's Concordance. There are also several smartphone apps that enable you to search in *Strong's Concordance*. Visit the app store on your smartphone, search for *Strong's Concordance*, and download one of these apps to begin your research.

8. Finally, test your understanding of the passage by paraphrasing the passage again in your own words.

Although paraphrasing may initially sound like a funny technique when you are trying to memorize a passage word-for-word, it is extremely difficult to memorize anything you do not understand. Paraphrasing the passage forces your brain to digest the thoughts behind the words and make sure that you fully understand what was written. When you are certain that you understand the heart of the passage, it will be much easier to commit the exact wording to memory.

Paul Marini

Actor,
Piercing Word Team Member

My favorite way to memorize Scripture is to initially record the particular passage I want to memorize on my phone or the GarageBand app. (Sometimes for my own listening pleasure I'll even put a little instrumental music behind it). Then I can listen to it on repeat any place, any time. I usually do this for a couple weeks. This helps me a lot to understand the overall themes and flow of what I'm memorizing. It also gets me familiar with the passage and makes the actual work of memorizing much easier.

My next step is to hand write the passage. This is very helpful because writing out each letter, word, sentence and thought engrains it into me in different ways and helps me memorize word perfectly! My last step is to literally get up, walk around and speak each thought out loud until it's memorized. Then I connect the thoughts together until it's all there! My biggest encouragement when memorizing is to seek to understand what you are memorizing and not bore yourself with the process.

Passive Memorization

"And the shepherds returned glorifying and praising God for all that they had heard and seen as it had been told them." My mother beamed as I finished quoting Luke 2:1–20 for the family during our annual Christmas gathering. It was a long-standing tradition in my family to read Luke 2 as our first activity when gathered together in the living room before exchanging presents with one another. And this year, I quoted it. I was about five or six years old, and the material was beyond my reading level. However, my mom had faithfully and consistently read Luke 2 to my brother and me every night before we went to bed since Thanksgiving so that, almost without trying, I had unwittingly memorized it. This is actually where my Bible memorization journey began.

AARON

This is what we call passive memorization. It is doing so much Pre-memorization that you actually passively memorize the passage. The same thing happens with music we listen to often or a favorite movie we like to quote; we passively memorize large portions of text without even trying. Why is this so easy? Because we have had an experience with the text that was exciting, funny, or emotionally memorable. You can harness these natural phenomena in your own Bible memorization experience.

Most of the time, even when using passive memorization, if you truly want to memorize anything word for word, you will need to do some amount of Active Memorization to fill in random "holes" in the text that were not passively filled in your memory. With a song, this is easily done simply by playing the song multiple times in a row and singing along with it. Do a few minutes of Active Memorization several days in a row, and you will have it memorized in what seems to be no time.

Let's Review!
Pre-memorization tactics:

- Read It
- Study It
- Record It
- Listen to It (either your own recording or audio Bible or Scripture song)
- Paraphrase It in your own words

Your progress through the memorization process

- ☑ Know Why
- <u>Know How</u>
- ☑ Plan It
- ☑ **UNDERSTAND IT**
- ☐ See It, Say It, Do It
- ☐ Review It
- ☐ Apply It
  (Repeat)

1. Was there a time you passively memorized something without even really trying? It could be a song, a phone number, a movie quote, or some random piece of information. Write down your experience. Why do you think you were able to memorize it so easily?

   _____

   _____

   _____

2. Fill out the "Understand It" section of your Plan of Attack in section B of Battle Resources.

3. Share your answers from the "Understand It" section of your Plan of Attack in the Warriors of the Word Facebook Group and with your accountability partner.

CHAPTER 6

The Art of War

Creating an Experience You Won't Forget

You shall therefore lay up these words of mine in your heart and in your soul, and you shall bind them as a sign on your hand, and they shall be as frontlets between your eyes. You shall teach them to your children, talking of them when you are sitting in your house, and when you are walking by the way, and when you lie down, and when you rise. You shall write them on the doorposts of your house and on your gates, that your days and the days of your children may be multiplied in the land that the Lord swore to your fathers to give them, as long as the heavens are above the earth.
~ Deuteronomy 11:18–21

Discovering Your Learning Style

"I hate memorizing."

Have these words ever come out of your mouth? Growing up, this was me. I hated memorizing. I hated coming to the end of a chapter in my history book only to moan at the intimidating list of random people, places, and dates I was expected to remember. I loved history, but I loved it for its stories. How could I be expected—weeks, months, and years later—to recall a list of details from an event I had never personally experienced?

EMILY

Here lies the key to memorization: *We must make memorization a personal, memorable experience.* As I remember this truth, I think back to my childhood once again and realize that there are certain things that I *do* still remember. For years after I graduated from high school, I could recall an impressive list of prepositions that I learned in grade school. I am now a mother of three and I can still sing some of the skip-counting songs my mom taught me in elementary school math.

> **SWORDPLAY TIP**
>
> We must make Bible memorization a personal, memorable experience.

Why? Now that I am a grown woman, why are there details from my schooling that I am astounded I can still remember, and yet other important historical dates and facts I am ashamed I can't recall?

It is now clear in my mind; the facts I *remember* are the facts I *experienced.* My mom, my siblings, and I listened to skip counting songs on a tape and then sang them together, sometimes laughing at the funny little tunes and rhymes that helped to jog our memories. We made a sort of "rap" out of the preposition list and competed to see who could successfully chant the entire list.

> **SWORDPLAY TIP**
>
> The things you remember are the things you experience.

I still can't rattle off all the American presidents or the list of important battles or ancient kings. Why? Because I simply tried to hammer them relentlessly into my bored brain. I did not *experience* these facts, so I cannot recall them.

So how do we go about creating an experience for ourselves while memorizing? Buckle up, because this is where it gets exciting.

Learning styles

Now it's your turn. What was your favorite class growing up? Why did you love it? Or conversely, what class was your least favorite and why did you dislike it? Take a moment to think about your answers.

I have found in my own life and in the lives of others that many subjects or classes are loved or hated depending on the teacher who taught it.

At the beginning of my Sophomore year, I distinctly remember dreading my chemistry class because I had so much trouble understanding algebra. I loved learning how things worked, but when upper-grade science became laden with complicated equations, I freaked out. However, I ended up thoroughly enjoying chemistry and even received an A in the class.

I attribute this success only to my amazing chemistry teacher. He let us build molecules with colorful molecule blocks and we did all sorts of crazy experiments. When it was time to decode complicated equations, he graded us based on the *process* we would use to find an answer, not just the solution itself. Not to mention he was a funny, lighthearted guy and we laughed a lot! My chemistry teacher made chemistry a *fun experience*.

Every good teacher will teach by using all three learning styles:

> **SWORDPLAY TIP**
>
> **If you are not having fun while memorizing the Bible, you are doing it wrong!**

1. **Auditory learning** is learning by *hearing*. The only way you can learn by hearing is if you speak aloud or listen to someone speaking aloud.

2. **Visual learning** is learning by *seeing*. This can be both seeing in the physical realm and "seeing" in your mind and imagination. For example, you could draw a picture on a piece of paper *or* you could paint a picture solely in your mind's eye.

3. **Kinesthetic learning** (or tactile learning) is hands-on learning. It is simply learning by *doing*.

Here is an easy, fun technique to remember all three learning styles when memorizing: *see it, say it, do it*.

Like my chemistry teacher, all *good* teachers teach by talking (auditory), by using textbooks, whiteboards, and illustrations (visual), and by assigning homework and fun, hands-on projects (kinesthetic). There are stronger and weaker ways to implement each learning style, which we will discuss later.

The next step is to discover what your primary learning style is. Everyone learns through all three learning styles, but every person learns best in one or possibly two of the learning styles. Once you discover your favorite and most effective learning style, you can focus your energies on using your top learning style and then apply the other two learning styles as supportive pillars to your one foundational style.

Remember when I asked you at the beginning of this section what your favorite and least favorite classes were in school? Did you make any discoveries about how your teacher taught, why you did or didn't like the class, or why you did or did not remember the information?

Perhaps you can't recall many specifics about your learning in school. Think of other information you have recently tried to digest at church, at work, or even when learning a new sport, game, or other skill. What made it memorable? What made it fun? What made it boring? What information can you still recall and why?

We highly encourage you to genuinely think about these questions. You will have the opportunity to write out your answers to these questions in the Learning Styles Quiz that you will take at the end of this chapter. Discovering the what and why behind these questions is crucial to discovering which learning style is most effective for you.

Aaron has always been primarily an auditory learner. However, as an adult, Aaron discovered that he also learns well by using the kinesthetic learning style.

His favorite technique is to act out the passage he is memorizing. As an example, let's say he was working on memorizing the following passage:

> Peter and John were going up to the temple at the hour of prayer, the ninth hour. And a man lame from birth was being carried, whom they laid daily at the gate of the temple that is called the Beautiful Gate to ask alms of those entering the temple. Seeing Peter and John about to go into the temple, he asked to receive alms. And Peter directed his gaze at him, as did John, and said, "Look at us." And he fixed his attention on them, expecting to receive something from them. But Peter said, "I have no silver and gold, but what I do have I give to you. In the name of Jesus Christ of Nazareth, rise up and walk!" And he took him by the right hand and raised him up, and immediately

his feet and ankles were made strong. And leaping up, he stood and began to walk, and entered the temple with them, walking and leaping and praising God. (Acts 3:1–8)

Let's say Aaron is memorizing this passage in our garage. To implement kinesthetic techniques, he would become the character of Peter and would picture the temple in the far corner of the garage. Then, turning his eyes to acknowledge invisible John who was walking beside him as he quoted, he would stride toward the imaginary Beautiful Gate and bend down to lay his hand gently upon the weed whacker (which looked remarkably like a lame beggar in his mind) and proclaim, "I have no silver and gold, but what I do have I give to you. In the name of Jesus Christ of Nazareth, rise up and walk!"

Did that picture of Aaron memorizing make you chuckle? I hope it did. The more you can make yourself smile, laugh, sigh, or even cry as you memorize, the more you will be able to *remember* what you memorize. Why? Simply because of this truth we will keep repeating—*you created an experience for yourself that you will not easily forget.* Step outside of your comfort zone and shake off your inhibitions about embarrassing yourself. There is no one watching you but you. So don't be embarrassed—just have *fun!*

Now that we have gone over an introductory example of a successful memorization technique, let's work through each major learning style and examine several creative approaches for implementing each one. Soon, you will have an entire arsenal of effective memory recall strategies ready to discharge at any time.

Before we begin, however, we would like to clarify something. You will notice that there is a lot of overlap in the techniques listed under each learning style. In other words, you will find some of them repeated as pertaining to two or even all three of the learning styles. This is because certain strategies utilize more than one learning style. Pay attention to these, because the more learning styles a specific technique incorporates, the more effective it will be.

And remember, if you are not having fun while you are doing your Active Memorization, you are doing it wrong! Be sure to try out the tactics in this chapter that sound the most fun to you first.

Auditory learning style tactics

Auditory techniques have to do with anything we hear with our ears. When memorizing *anything, always read the material aloud.* Don't read silently and don't whisper! If at all possible, let your voice fill the room that you are in. This commands your ears, your mind, and the rest of your body to pay attention and conveys to your easily distracted self that you are fully committed and that the material at hand is important and engaging.

SWORDPLAY TIP

Never memorize silently.

In addition to reading the passage out loud, a slightly more creative auditory technique is to **voice record your passage.** This enables you to listen to the passage over and over again anywhere, anytime, and any place. You can simply loop the recording as you go about your daily tasks, either preparing your mind for more intense memorization later or reinforcing a previously memorized passage. This technique is most effective in the Pre-memorization and Review portions of the Piercing Word Bible Memorization Process.

SWORDPLAY TIP

Try voice recording your passage and listening to it while driving, doing dishes, or folding laundry.

Music is an especially effective form of memorizing text. Aaron recently had the privilege to speak with J. David Newquist of Word for Word Ministries, Inc. Newquist has successfully set the entire New Testament to music, and he is currently working on producing all of it. At the time of the publishing of this book, Newquist has produced the first chapter of all twenty-seven books of the New Testament and several full books, like Philippians, Ephesians, and 1 Thessalonians. Once he finishes production of the New Testament, he has plans to do the same with the Old Testament. You can find out more about his resources in section 2 of The Arsenal. Newquist shared with Aaron how historically, Hindus would memorize the entirety of their sacred text (or Vedas) syllable by syllable. This was done for 1000 years before their sacred text was ever written down. Here's the kicker: the Hindu sacred text is three times the length of our entire Christian Bible. How did they do it? Through chanting. They used musical rhythms and melodic concepts to memorize one hundred thousand verses of content. In Christian history, similar musical methods have been used in memorizing Scripture. For instance, monks memorized all the psalms. Some Christian traditions have liturgically chanted specific sections of the New Testament from the first century until now. Newquist even went so far as to say that music is the single most effective way to memorize Scripture, and that this has been proven historically by some of these examples.

You can harness the power of music to memorize Scripture. In fact, there are enough Scripture music resources listed in section 2 of The Arsenal for you to complete nearly every memorization track listed in chapter 3 primarily using Scripture songs. You can use these resources to help you find songs for almost every portion of your Marching Orders (Battle Resources: A). If you love music and find music to be one of your favorite ways to memorize, you can simply purchase or download some Scripture music to listen to and memorize as you go about your normal daily routine.

SWORDPLAY TIP

Harness the power of music to memorize Scripture.

If you are musically inclined, you do not even have to use the resources provided in The Arsenal to sing the Scripture. You can enjoy being creative and **set the passage you are memorizing to your own music or melody and sing it.** This could be as simple as setting the words to a familiar tune or as complex as composing an original melody for the passage. I fall somewhere in between both extremes . . .I love to sing, but I don't have the necessary musical knowledge to easily compose a musical piece. However, I will sometimes make up my own tune for a verse I am memorizing and record it on the voice recorder app on my cell phone. This gives me an auditory reference for my melody, even though I lack a written score. Then I just sing along with myself until it is so stuck in my head that I can't forget it.

Using **word associations** is technically an auditory technique, but it often has visual or kinesthetic mixed in. I am not a strong auditory learner. Yet, because the word association method is easily mixed with visual and kinesthetic techniques, I have enjoyed using this auditory strategy. For example, I employed word associations in the memorization of the following list of cities and countries from Acts 2:

> There were dwelling in Jerusalem Jews, devout men from every nation under heaven. And at this sound the multitude came together, and they were bewildered, because each one was hearing them speak in his own language. And they were amazed and astonished, saying, "Are not all these who are speaking Galileans? And how is it that we hear, each of us in his own native language? Parthians and Medes and Elamites and residents of Mesopotamia, Judea and Cappadocia, Pontus and Asia, Phrygia and Pamphylia, Egypt and the parts of Libya belonging to Cyrene, and visitors from Rome, both Jews and proselytes, Cretans and Arabians—we hear them telling in our own tongues the mighty works of God." (Acts 2:5–11)

Aaron and I had to memorize this list of places as part of our Acts 2 Scripture Script. We performed it in the place it actually happened during one of our annual Piercing Word tours to Israel. I was responsible for memorizing about half of this list. I was at first bewildered on how to go about memorizing these countries and cities that I was so unfamiliar with until I realized that many of the

VICTORY STORY

Hope Kemp
Wife, Mother,
Scripture Music Composer

My favorite way to memorize Scripture is by putting it into a song. I am a musician and songwriter, and so setting ideas to music is a natural exercise and repose for me. I memorize Scripture by putting it to music because a song can rattle around inside the head a lot longer, and resurrect at opportune times, much easier than words without music can. One thing I would encourage everyone to do when memorizing is to have desire, purpose, and intent for wanting to memorize that particular passage. Also, practice your memorizing while doing something you love—especially if it's creative or artistic.

strange names reminded me of other words that *were* familiar to me. For example, Judea made me think of Jews, so I made a motion of a Jewish kippah on my head (the kind of cap that traditional Jewish men and boys wear) to jog my memory. Cappadocia? I grabbed the bill of my invisible baseball cap and the odd city name came right back to me. Phrygia sounded like frigid, so I said that word like I was shivering. Pamphilia sounded like a pamphlet, so I pretended to unfold and look at a pamphlet as I repeated Pamphilia. I of course did not use my motions in our actual performance. By then I didn't need to—I had already effectively taught my brain to associate each city or country with a specific word. As I recalled the familiar word and motion in my mind's eye, the actual place came racing back to my tongue.

One of our favorite ways to test our memories is through the **technique of quoting a Scripture passage in different voices, accents, intentions, or inflections.** Changing your inflection as you memorize or quote is the easiest way to mix up your vocal pattern and explore the text in new ways with each repetition. Try it. Simply emphasize a different word each time as you quote the phrase "For God so loved the world . . ."

The next level would be to use **different intentions** as you memorize or quote. Some examples of different intentions could be happy, sad, hopeful, in love, angry, pleading, bitter, sarcastic, and endless others!. Using these simple actions can also be a unique way of studying the passage as you explore all the possible ways it could have been intended to be read or said.

We believe using various inflections and intentions as you do your Active Memorization is a *must.* If you do not do this, you are in danger of using muscle memory to memorize how the words and phrases feel in your mouth as you say them, rather than using your brain to memorize the actual thoughts behind the words. The latter is far more potent and lasting. Another vocal layer to add is quoting the passage in a **favorite foreign accent**, such as British, French, Chinese, Indian, Italian, Southern, and so on. This is especially helpful during Maintenance Review when you have already said the passage many times, and you need a fresh perspective on the passage in order to keep your review time creative and interesting.

Yet another fun strategy to keep things vocally interesting is quoting your memorized verses in a **character voice**. You can pick a general type of character, such as a mom, a sports coach, a little child, an elderly woman, a cheerleader, a cowboy, and so on. You can also go more specific and choose a character from a movie, such as Edna Mode from *The Incredibles*, Elmo from *Sesame Street*, or even a character like Mrs. Lynde from *Anne of Green Gables*. Once again, these character voices are probably best utilized in Maintenance Review rather than Active Memorization or Solidification Review as you do not want to distract yourself from the goal of memorization and retention with too many bizarre choices before getting the content under your belt.

> **SWORDPLAY TIP**
>
> Become a character! Imitate your favorite cartoon character while quoting your passage or mimic your favorite foreign accent.

Some people may feel uncomfortable implementing these exercises with the Holy Scriptures. It may feel almost sacrilegious to "play" with the Word of God. We understand these sentiments. However, we would also like to gently confront this concern. We as the church seem to most often interact with the Word of God in monotone voices with little to no expression in our faces. We often—dare I say it?—make the Word of God seem *boring*. Making God's Word seem boring is perhaps even more offensive than having fun with it. God knows our hearts. If your heart is to make light of Scripture and to make fun of the Bible, then of course God will not be honored through your actions. However, if your heart is to engage with God and his Word on a more intensive level and to make memorization of his Word a fun and engaging experience, then he will be honored.

Before we move on, we want to mention that there is a valuable psychological benefit to this exercise as well. Most people memorize in only one vocal pattern. They repeat the phrases in the same manner, with the same intonations every single time they say it. Although this method may bring immediate gratification when you are able to repeat back a phrase quickly while doing Active Memorization, it can be detrimental to effective long-term memory retention.

We have discovered firsthand how tempting it is to keep the same vocal pattern when memorizing. However, when you memorize in only one vocal pattern, you set yourself up for difficulty. When reviewing that passage in the future, there is no guarantee that each phrase will verbally come out exactly as when you first memorized it. If the words come out differently during review later on, you may draw a memory blank, because your brain cannot recall the words without the associated muscle memory of the vocal intonations. Having fun with different inflections and intentions as you memorize and review purposefully mixes up vocal patterns and helps to cement the memorization of the actual thoughts and truths of the passage in your brain. Using accents and character voices as you review can be a great test of true memorization and can cement the concepts and truths even more deeply in your mind. To get you started, here is a short list of different types of characters, tactics, and accents you could use when memorizing or reviewing your passage.

CHARACTERS	INTENTIONS	ACCENTS
• Cowboy	• To love	• Cockney
• Grandpa/Grandma	• To beg	• British Proper
• Little kid	• To test	• French
• Surfer	• To hurt	• Irish
• Cheerleader	• To admit	• Scottish
• The President	• To impress	• Australian
• Homeless person	• To challenge	• New York
• Army Commander	• To entertain	• American
	• To advise	• Southern

Try saying 1 Thessalonians 5:16–18 in three completely different voices by picking from the ways listed here.

Rejoice always, pray without ceasing, give thanks in all circumstances; for this is the will of God in Christ Jesus for you. (1 Thessalonians 5:16–18)

Using different vocal inflections when reading or quoting Scripture can actually enhance your study of God's Word. We often forget that the Bible was written by real people with real emotions. Playing around with different inflections and intentions for a specific passage is almost like slipping a different lens on God's Word. Sometimes you will discover a lens that makes the colors of Scripture pop like never before. I will never forget a moment when I was studying 1 Corinthians 4. I was playing around with different intentions as I read the passage and I tried saying the verses with a sarcastic tone.

> Already you have all you want! Already you have become rich! Without us you have become kings! And would that you did reign, so that we might share the rule with you!

As I read verse 8 aloud that way, I literally gasped aloud as my understanding of the verse suddenly clicked into place. Verses I had never understood before suddenly made sense. Paul had been writing *sarcastically* to the church to make a point! Never before would I have thought to impose a sarcastic tone on one of our renowned biblical apostles. But he was a real person, speaking to others, and trying to drive a point home to them through his sarcastic comment. You may be surprised how much deeper you can dive into Scripture through this exercise.

Let's review the AUDITORY learning style tactics
- Read it aloud
- Record it and listen to it
- Sing it to a familiar tune or compose your own
- Make word associations
- Say it with different inflections, intentions, accents, and character voices

Visual learning style tactics

Visual learning techniques always have something to do with seeing. This could be seeing through our physical eyes, but it could also mean seeing through our mind's eye. I am primarily a kinesthetic learner, but visual learning comes in as a close second, particularly because visual and kinesthetic learning often go hand-in-hand. Just a reminder: as you learn these visual learning strategies, you should always say the passage out loud in order to constantly and consistently *see it, say it, and do it* during Active Memorization.

The simplest and most obvious visual technique to apply is **reading the scriptural text**. Your eyes are visually seeing the words on the page and this

> SWORDPLAY TIP
>
> The techniques for visual learning can be as endless as your creativity.

helps to engage your brain. Start with this technique, but don't end there; the techniques for visual learning can be as endless as your creativity.

A simple next step would be to **write out the passage or type it** on a computer. This technique is both kinesthetic and visual, which, although it is simple, makes it an advantageous technique for some people.

You can take this tactic a step further by writing your memory verses on note cards. Many people enjoy this memorization technique. It gets your body actively involved and creates a pocket-sized reference for you to take on the go. This is helpful because it enables you to use your random margin minutes to review your Scripture memory passages.

> SWORDPLAY TIP
>
> Write your memory verses on note cards for a pocket-sized reference to take on the go.

Now let's get creative in our mind's eye in order to **create mental pictures** with the following passage:

> You cast me into the deep,
>   into the heart of the seas,
>   and the flood surrounded me;
> all your waves and your billows
>   passed over me.
> Then I said, "I am driven away
>   from your sight;
> yet I shall again look
>   upon your holy temple."
> (Jonah 2:3–4)

Let's take this passage phrase by phrase and create some plays on words to make a fun and crazy mental picture. For "you cast me into the deep," picture yourself on the end of God's fishing line as he casts you into the deep end of a pool. For "into the heart of the seas," suddenly you are deep into a giant red heart that is submerged in the water. As you think of "the flood surrounded me," picture the water flooding over you on God's fishing line inside the giant heart. "All your waves and your billows passed over me" might bring to mind mermaids waving at you while blowing strong billows upon you through their pursed lips. In "I am driven away from your sight," the giant heart now has a steering wheel and wheels, as you desperately try to drive away from God's gaze. For "yet I shall again look upon your holy temple," suddenly you see God's welcoming temple gleaming in the distant sky and you stop trying to drive away because you are filled with hope.

Does this mental picture strike you as utterly absurd? If so, perfect! Honestly, the weirder it is, the more you will remember it. Things that make us laugh or things that our brains find bizarre or unique are the things that strike our minds as worth remembering. This is a strong visual memorization approach. It can also be used to tie together two seemingly unrelated verses or sections of Scripture you are having trouble tying together.

SWORDPLAY TIP

The more bizarre it is, the more you will remember it.

Another technique of using bizarre mental images to memorize Scripture (or anything else you want to memorize) is by using the Loci Method, an absurd and creative approach that will have you laughing and will glue information in your memory for good. Esther Eaton, one of our book editors and a former Piercing Word intern, explains her experience with the Loci Method below. First she will describe it as it regards memorizing a random list of grocery items and then as it pertains to memorizing Scripture:

> My go-to memory technique began with reading about a tragic dinner party narrated by Cicero. Ancient Greek poet Simonides stepped outside the banquet, and while he was away the roof collapsed. Simonides helped rescuers identify

the victims by recalling where each person had been sitting. He realized the power of associating place and name, and taught orators to imagine the points of their speeches in physical locations.

I first heard about this method, now called the Loci Method, through journalist Joshua Foer's book *Moonwalking with Einstein*, about his journey through the world of competitive memory. Years later thanks to that book, I still have a jar of pickles next to my mailbox, a kiddie pool of cottage cheese on my front step, and three women hula-hooping on my kitchen table. Yes, these imagined images are useless to me. No, I can't get rid of them. If you, too, want a curated list of strange objects stuck in your brain, I recommend Foer's book.

Foer explains it better than I can, but here's a rough summary of the Loci Method: Convert the list you're trying to memorize into a series of striking visual images. Involve action and other senses if possible. (For instance, I dip my hand in the pool of cottage cheese—and then reflexively gag at the lumpy slime.) As you create the images, place them one by one into a space you are intimately familiar with. I used my childhood home. To recall the list, imagine yourself walking through the space, encountering the objects one by one.

I start at my mailbox where I knock on the jar of pickles, walk up the driveway and through the front door after swishing the cottage cheese, then into the kitchen where I wave at the hula hoopers. This method keeps me from skipping items; I always pass the front step on my way from mailbox to kitchen, so I never forget the cottage cheese.

If you place items of a list like this, you won't forget them. Trust me, I've tried.

Maybe this reminds you of storing information in a mind palace, as in BBC's show *Sherlock*. The difference between the classic Loci Method and a mind palace is that you invent your mind palace, constructing every detail, while the Loci Method uses a real location you're already familiar with. I have a mind palace, and I enjoy it. But unless you already have one, building enough detail to make it useful for memorization is a lot of extra work. The Loci Method makes use of what you already know instead of inventing one more thing to remember.

It's easiest to use the Loci Method with a list of objects, but you can also apply its principles to a chunk of text. Just make each phrase of that chunk visual and specific and set it in motion. Think of memorizing as building a Rube Goldberg machine. Visualize the concepts in the text as objects in motion, each triggering the next. With any piece missing, the machine stops moving. If you want to be word perfect, justify to yourself why each word is crucial to its piece of the machine. I admit, this is a little more complex than leaving cottage cheese on your front step. It requires you to deeply ponder a passage, training your mind to follow its reasoning and treat every detail as significant. But it makes Scripture stick, and over time it makes you automatically attentive to the nuance of every passage you read. In my mind, that is worth the effort. Thanks, Simonides.

Another fun visual technique is to create an original artistic rendering of the passage with pictures interlacing the text, like the ones pictured on the next two pages.

Therefore, if anyone is in Christ, he is a NEW creation. The OLD HAS passed away; Behold, the NEW HAS COME. All This is from God, who THROUGH Christ reconciled us to himself and GAVE US the Ministry of Reconciliation.

2 Corinthians 5:17-18

Artwork by Hannah Orneles

Rejoice ALWAYS, I Thess. 5:16-18

pray Without Ceasing,

Give THANKS in all

Circumstances; For THIS

is the WILL of GOD in CHRIST

JESUS for You.

Artwork by Hannah Orneles

Or you can casually doodle the passage into pictures without text like Adelina. Here is her Victory Story.

VICTORY STORY

Adelina Wenger
Wife, Actress,
Piercing Word Team Member

My favorite way to memorize God's Word is to create doodles and little pictures that represent each sentence or even each word. I start by breaking down the passage I am going to memorize into manageable sections, often sections that focus on one theme or topic. Then I start with only the first sentence. I get a blank notebook and pencil and start drawing a doodle for each word. I do not put pressure on myself to create beautiful or perfect little drawings! This would only make the process stressful and hinder memorization. Sometimes the doodles are easy to come up with; sometimes they're extremely difficult. For example, whenever I see the word "be" I draw a little cartoon bumble bee. Words like "propitiation" or "righteousness" are a different challenge and I just do my best to draw a little picture that will make sense to my mind. Words like "the," "then," and "therefore" or phrases like "that they were" are especially difficult to draw because they are so basic. So I often just write the first letter of those words instead of drawing a picture for each one so that I give my mind a clue as to what the words are.

In a way, this is like a puzzle or secret code that I create for myself. Once I finish drawing a section of Scripture, I go back and look only at my drawings and try to remember what each picture represents. This is a fun challenge that starts to connect and cement the Scripture passage in my brain. I continue to use the pictures for recalling words until I am slowly able to recite the passage without looking at the pictures at all. Then I will ask a friend to hold a copy of the passage and check my accuracy as I recite from memory.

(continued)

After I finish the initial phase of drawings, I may go back and draw a single picture that represents the entire section of Scripture I have memorized. This is a way to make larger chunks of Scripture more manageable for my brain so that I can remember the order of each section as I perform or recite the entire passage. This is possible because once I fully memorize a passage, I no longer need to visualize every picture for every word in order to remember the passage. The single, thematic picture is all I need to spark my memory of an entire section. The pictures are used to make those initial connections in my brain and after that is complete, I often only use the thematic pictures I create in order to review the passage.

Drawing the Scriptures takes a lot of time. However, I've found that it significantly speeds up my memorization process and causes the Scripture passage to be more firmly rooted in my mind than any other method.

Once I have memorized a passage of Scripture, I never look at it the same way again. It becomes like a dear friend. Memorization forms a special intimacy with the words of Scripture that cannot be obtained by casual reading alone. Memorization causes you to spend time with and meditate upon Scripture in a way that no other method can. In the process, you are also growing in intimacy with God himself as you intentionally internalize his Word.

Lastly, another visual technique to utilize is **object association**. The example a few pages back of Aaron acting out the story of Peter healing a lame man at the temple is an example of the use of this technique. Aaron associated different parts of the passage with different areas of the garage or different items in the garage. Because of this association, if he were to go back to those spots or even just visualize them in his mind, the story he committed to memory would come flooding back.

Let's review the VISUAL learning style tactics

- Read it
- Type it
- Write it
- Create word pictures
- Make an artistic rendering of the passage
- Use an object association

Kinesthetic learning style tactics

Last but not least, let's discuss my personal favorite learning style, kinesthetic. Kinesthetic learning, or tactile learning, is what we call hands-on learning. It includes any technique that involves *doing* or becoming physically active as you learn or memorize. This is perhaps the most effective of the learning styles simply because *doing* usually involves more of the senses than any other style and more easily creates an *experience* that you can remember, which is always the goal when memorizing. As another reminder, even as you practice these kinesthetic techniques, be sure to also say the passage out loud in order to make it a true *see it, say it, do it* experience.

The simplest technique to involve kinesthetic learning when memorizing is the same as our first visual suggestions: *type it or write it.* Yes, this is visual because you see it with your eyes, but it is also kinesthetic because you are using your hands to write or type it.

> **SWORDPLAY TIP**
>
> To make memorization a fun and memorable experience, we must become like children again.

My personal favorite kinesthetic technique is using **hand motions**. For some reason, we often think of hand motions as being only for children. We try hard to make Bible memorization fun and engaging for the little ones among us. But once we get past elementary school, we often resort to boring drills and try to just "hammer it in" our brains. Let's become like children again!

Hand motions can involve just your hands or can involve even more of your body. These can range from simple motions that even a

toddler could grasp, to sign language, to pantomime, to something so fluid and graceful that it is more like a lyrical interpretive dance. *Hand motions can be whatever you want them to be*. There's no right or wrong when it comes to creating hand motions; whatever helps you learn and whatever you think is fun is the right choice.

Acting it out is exactly what it sounds like. Remember, become a child again. Create a memorable experience for yourself. Choose props and engage your mind with object association. Use voices, accents, and intentions to become the biblical characters and truly experience the story or text.

> **SWORDPLAY TIP**
>
> Get your body moving while memorizing! Find methods to physically experience the text.

Even **taking a walk** while memorizing or quoting gets your body moving and you can potentially utilize some object associations on your walk. For some people, acting it out with props might be more effective than this, but walking is usually much more effective than simply standing still and memorizing.

Who doesn't find songs easier to memorize than chunks of text? **Sing the Scripture!** We discussed this technique in our Auditory Learning Styles section, but singing can also be a strong kinesthetic technique. You could make it even stronger by singing while doing hand motions.

Maybe putting Scripture to a melody intimidates you, but you would have fun **rapping the passage or making it into a rhythmic chant.** This is a simpler, more mild form of melody that still aids in memorization and in creating a fun experience.

Do you love to dance? Try **dancing Scripture.** What this means is that you choreograph movement to each phrase, word, or main idea in the passage you are memorizing. Record the passage on your phone, then dance to it as you listen to the recording, quoting along with yourself as you dance. This is basically a more complex, artsy approach to hand motions and utilizes the power of associating words with movement.

Derek Martin

VICTORY STORY

Dance Instructor, Gymnast,
Piercing Word Actor and Choreographer

I originally began memorizing with all of the usual methods. Repeating lines out loud, writing the phrases over and over again, and listening to the portions of Scripture through the Bible app. They all worked for me, but I didn't feel like I got the Scripture locked into my heart and written there. With those methods, the words I had been studying and memorizing didn't seem to apply to my life. They didn't come to mind in situations where I would have needed them too.

It wasn't until I started to marry my love of dance with my Scripture memory practice that the Word was really written on the tablet of my heart.

My mentor and I began the process of memorizing 1 Peter at that time, since I was in rehearsals for that piece with Piercing Word. I used a lot of hand motions to help me memorize. They worked surprisingly well for me and I had to spend much less time on the work of memorizing. It still felt like work, though. As he and I got through chapters 1 and 2 and moved onto chapter 3, I asked myself, "Why don't I just dance it?"

I didn't have a good answer as to why I had not. After all, nobody would have to see the dance. So, I started involving my whole body in the memorization process. Being a dancer and choreographer, this helped immensely and memorization did not feel like work at all. It suddenly clicked! Why hadn't I been doing this all along? It was during that process that I also remembered my experience that I've written about above. The light bulb turned on to full brightness. "I should have been doing this for years!" I exclaimed to myself.

Gaming the Scriptures is an extremely fun and effective approach to memorizing kinesthetically. We highly recommend three main techniques, though there are others out there as well. These gaming strategies are especially keen for people who like word games or word puzzles or people who consider themselves to be less artistically inclined. Multiple smartphone Bible memory apps, like VerseLocker and Fighter Verses, have been created based on these memorization techniques. So feel free to download one of these apps to help you implement these methods, or you can just practice them the old-fashioned way.

The first gaming technique is simple yet cleverly engaging. Write the passage with an erasable writing implement like a pencil on paper, a dry erase marker on a white board, or chalk on a chalkboard. Once you have written the passage, read it out loud a couple of times. Then erase a few words and read it again. If that goes well, erase a few more words and recite it again. Continue until you have erased every word from your writing surface. If you can quote the verse now with no visual prompt, you have successfully memorized it. Now you can move on to the next verse. On the next page, there is an example of what that can look like with 1 Thessalonians 5:16-18. Read through the verses out loud each time you see it written out. As more words disappear, challenge yourself to not look back at the full verse, and see if you can remember the missing words.

The second gaming technique we recommend is perhaps most effective for review, but it can also be used during Active Memorization. To use this technique as a part of your Active Memorization, try writing out the first letter of each word in the verses on note cards. In other words, "For God so loved the world . . ." would read "FGSLTW . . ." and so on. Begin by reading the actual passage a few times out loud, then switch to looking only at your note card acronym as you try saying the verse several times with only the first letter prompts. Then look up and try saying it several times without any prompts. When you complete that verse, move on to the next verse and repeat these same steps. Try remembering 1 Thessalonians 5:16–18 by reading this acronym below:

RAPWCGTIACFTITWOGICJFY

Rejoice always,
pray without ceasing,
give thanks in all circumstances;
for this is the will of God in
Christ Jesus for you.

1 THESSALONIANS 5:16-18

Rejoice _____,
_____ without ceasing,
give thanks in all _____;
for this is the _____ of God in
_____ _____ for you.

1 THESSALONIANS 5:16-18

_____ _____,
_____ without _____,
give _____ in all _____;
for _____ is the _____ of ___ in
_____ _____ for ___.

1 THESSALONIANS 5:16-18

_____ _____,
_____ _____ _____,
_____ _____ __ ___ _____;
__ ____ __ ___ __ __ ___ __
_____ _____ ___ ___.

1 THESSALONIANS 5:16-18

While reviewing, try writing the first letter of each word in the verse while quoting. It is attainable to write the first letter of each word at the same speed as you speak the passage. It is also a great technique to check yourself on your memorization to ensure you are word perfect. After quoting and writing the first letter of each word, compare your acronym with the actual text to see if you skipped, switched, or paraphrased anything.

One time we were leading a *Warriors of the Word* small group at our church where we studied and memorized the book of Colossians together. During the course of the class, our friends Nathanael and Alyssa Waite and their kids decided to construct an acronym using the first letter of each word for the entire chapter of Colossians 3. They proceeded to write the entire acronym on a series of note cards and hang them in sequential order around the entire kitchen. This was a fun family review technique to get them all reviewing their chapter together.

In addition to acronyms being used to remember the order of words in a verse, they can also be used for remembering the order of sections in a chapter or book. My dad, Steve Douglass, has used this technique when memorizing Scripture. When he was memorizing the Sermon on the Mount from Matthew 5–7, he created an acronym from the first key word in each section in Matthew 5. So the sections in Matthew 5:21–48 became the following: "M" for Murder, "A" for Adultery, "D" for Divorce, "S" for Swear, "E" for Eye, "L" for Love.

VICTORY STORY

Mandee Kline
Former Piercing Word Intern

My favorite way to memorize Scripture is by writing it out. I will write out the verses in different fonts. Once I'm feeling more confident with the material, I then write down the first letter of each word. The letters easily became short words! It's basically an acrostic!

He then was able to remember the entire order of this section by remembering the acronym they created: MAD SEL. Along with his acronyms, he created mental images that helped him remember the thought process and meaning of each section.

The third way to game your Active Memorization is to **time yourself** while you use some of the other strategies listed in this chapter. Aaron loves to utilize a timer when doing Active Memorization. The first time you try this out, you will need to make a guess of how long it will take you to Actively Memorize the selected passage for the day. For instance, you may guess that you can memorize three verses in fifteen minutes. If you were too ambitious with this goal and three verses took you thirty minutes, then you will have a better idea of how to set your timing goal for the following day accordingly. As you continue this practice, you can begin to try to beat your previous times. This is a fun exercise for Aaron because he is a competitive person. He grew up as a competitive swimmer, which is all about racing yourself and beating your personal best times from the past, so timing his memorization works well for him.

SWORDPLAY TIP

Set a timer and race yourself.

If you are not a competitive person and using a timer for your Active Memorization stresses you out, rather than being challenging and fun, by all means, do not do it. Remember, if you are not having fun while memorizing Scripture, you are doing something wrong. With every suggestion in this chapter, you have to find what works for you.

Let's review the KINESTHETIC learning style tactics
- Type it
- Write it
- Use hand motions (add word associations if helpful)
- Act it
- Take a walk
- Sing it
- Rap it
- Dance it
- Game it

AARON

Active Memorization Ground Rules

Now that you are armed with lots of creative strategies for your memorization maneuvers, it's time to learn the ground rules of Active Memorization. There are certain things that everyone should do during Active Memorization.

Remember: Active Memorization is a one-time memorization experience with a specific and attainable goal and set time frame when you are alone with no distractions, using all your focus and attention.

Use all three learning styles—see it, say it, do it

The most important thing to keep in mind as you experiment with these different learning styles and techniques is to remember that *you are a teacher of yourself.* You, as the teacher, have the ability to either teach the material to yourself in an exciting or boring way. If you are bored when memorizing Scripture, it is your own fault. Be a good teacher of yourself and engage your brain and body with *all three learning styles—see it, say it, do it.* If you do this, you will create a fun experience that engages so many of your senses that you will have trouble forgetting what you memorize.

SWORDPLAY TIP

Be a good teacher of yourself—see it, say it, and do it!

Memorize phrase by phrase

Reading and listening to your entire chosen passage is great for Pre-memorization. However, during the Active Memorization stage you will need to memorize phrase by phrase. For instance, a single verse may contain anywhere from one phrase to as many as ten phrases. During Active Memorization, we are going to creatively analyze and intentionally memorize each phrase one by one. This gives your mind very small and attainable pieces of information to digest and store in your memory. It's just like the answer to the colloquial question, "How do you eat an elephant? One bite at a time."

As an example, let's say you are doing Active Memorization on three verses for fifteen minutes. This should be your process during that fifteen minutes:

1. Read through all three verses out loud once or twice to get them in your mind as a whole.

2. See, say, and do the first phrase of the first verse until you can say it without looking at the text. If you are using your creativity in your seeing, saying, and doing, this should go rather quickly.

3. See, say, and do the second phrase by itself until you can say it without looking at the text.

4. See, say and do phrases one and two together. It may help to look at the text the first time you put them together, then try to say the two phrases together without looking at the text. If you struggle at first with putting two phrases together, think about the author's intent in putting these two phrases side by side as you continue to repeat them together.

5. See, say, and do the third phrase by itself until you can say it without looking at the text.

6. See, say, and do all three phrases together until you can say them in succession without looking at the text.

7. Continue in this manner until you can say the entirety of all three verses in succession without looking.

8. Repeat all three verses creatively as a whole three more times.

You are finished with your Active Memorization for the day! Now these three verses are ready to start the review process tomorrow.

You should be able to move quickly through these steps once you get used to using the creative techniques described in this book. This can be a very fast paced and fun creative experience. The key is to be sure you stay focused during your entire Active Memorization stage. When I do Active Memorization, I literally never stop speaking the entire time as I move from phrase to phrase and creatively act out each line. You will be amazed at how much creative repetition you can pack into just fifteen minutes when working this way.

If you are bored with repeating your verses during or after your Active Memorization, you have not been creative enough and need to try implementing a few of the memorization tactics mentioned earlier in this chapter.

If you are memorizing a longer passage in one sitting, like one that has two full paragraphs, it can be helpful to memorize the first paragraph phrase by phrase, and then memorize the second paragraph phrase by phrase without going back to the first paragraph after each phrase in the second paragraph. Complete Active Memorization on the second paragraph, then tie both paragraphs together creatively in your memory.

Never memorize silently

One of the biggest pitfalls that we have seen interfering with success in memorization is trying to memorize silently. When most people in our modern culture try to memorize something, the first thing they do is read the passage silently multiple times and then look up and see if they can repeat the words silently in their own brain. This is clearly not being a good teacher of yourself. It incorporates only one weak visual learning technique. For 95 percent of people, memorizing silently is a painful and ineffective way to memorize Scripture. I would compare it to stabbing yourself in the eye. I avoid it at all costs. Almost inevitably, when we meet someone who says, "I have a terrible memory," we discover that they have only attempted silent memorization. If you do not memorize out loud, you are neglecting the easiest way to incorporate the auditory learning style into your memorization process. As a disclaimer, I have met some people that say that they can successfully memorize things silently. If you are one of those people, you are blessed with a high visual learning capacity and are probably naturally incorporating some of the strong visual and kinesthetic techniques described in this chapter. Even still, if you are part of the 5 percent of people who memorize well silently, I dare you to try incorporating memorizing out loud to speed up your process. Three learning styles is always superior to two.

Pray before you begin

It is always a great idea to invite the Author of the Bible into your Bible memorization time. The times that I have spent asking the Lord's presence to be upon me while memorizing have been well worth it. When I pray and invite him into the space with me, my time spent memorizing becomes sweet communion with my Savior. When I have neglected to pray before beginning, memorization can easily become a chore or just another "to do" item rather than sweet time with Jesus.

Sit up straight or stand

One early morning, when I was memorizing the New Testament, I began my memorization time by curling up in the recliner in our living room. About thirty minutes later, I had gotten nowhere. *What is wrong with me?* I thought to myself. *Yesterday, I successfully memorized fifteen new verses in thirty minutes, and today I can't seem to get anywhere.* I decided this passage was not going to get the best of me. I sat up straight, put my feet flat on the ground and leaned forward slightly. I was determined to conquer this passage. Immediately, I started having success. The next day, I took it a step further and decided to stand while memorizing. Even though I was using a heavy study Bible for my memorization time, I decided it was worth the experiment. That day, I memorized my daily verse quota in record time. Ever since then, I have determined to always do my Active Memorization while standing. Any other position is less efficient for me.

This simple practice makes a *profound* difference in the practice of Active Memorization. Since that time, I have literally found myself memorizing twice as fast when I sit straight versus slouching or reclining. And I memorize three times faster when I stand than when I sit. Both sitting up straight and standing tell your body that you are invested and involved in what you are doing. It tells your brain that what you are doing is important. You literally receive more blood flow to the brain. Avoid doing Active Memorization while reclining, slouching, or lying down. Lazy posture is almost as destructive to memorization as memorizing silently.

Memorize the thoughts, not just the words

This point is twofold. You must first understand what the text is saying from thought to thought. So often when we set out to memorize something, we are in such a hurry to get the words memorized that we don't slow down enough to think about what we are saying. This was covered more extensively in the previous chapter on Pre-memorization.

Second, when you go about Active Memorization, you must not get hung up on memorizing individual words. The human brain does a much better job of memorizing text in a thought-for-thought format than word-for-word. Joshua Foer also confirms this truth in his book entitled *Moonwalking with Einstein.* That is *not* to say that you should not worry about saying the right words as you do your Active Memorization. The more you say the right words, the more your mind and mouth will be accustomed to them, and the better your recitations will get each time. However, you should never let a small word or two pause your memorization or recitation if you know what the correct next thought is. Push past the uncertain word choice, and test your thought-for-thought recall *first*. Word-for-word recall perfection should only be focused on during review (especially with a review partner as we will discuss in detail in the chapter on review). Before you can successfully memorize something word for word, you must first memorize it thought for thought. (See chapter 8 for more thoughts on this topic.)

Experience it

We remember only a small percentage of what we read, but we remember a high percentage of what we experience. In this chapter, you have learned how to create experiences around the Word of God during your Active Memorization process.

Have fun

Different things are fun for different people. We are confident that, no matter who you are or what your likes and dislikes are, you will find tactics in this book that you will enjoy and can use to have fun while memorizing.

If you follow these essential tips when you are doing your Active Memorization, you will find Bible memorization to be a blessed and rewarding experience.

Let's Review
Active Memorization Ground Rules
- Use all three learning styles
- Memorize phrase by phrase
- Never memorize silently
- Pray before you begin
- Sit up straight or stand
- Memorize the thoughts, not just the words
- Experience it
- Have fun

Active Memorization Tactics to Try

<u>SEE IT</u>	<u>SAY IT</u>	<u>DO IT</u>
Write it	Sing it	Use hand motions
Draw it	Record it	Dance it
Game it	Vary inflection/intention	Act it
Acronyms	Use accents/voices	Type it

Your progress through the memorization process

- ☑ Know Why
- <u>Know How</u>
  - ☑ Plan It
  - ☑ Understand It
  - ☑ **SEE IT, SAY IT, DO IT**
  - ☐ Review It
  - ☐ Apply It
  - (Repeat)

1. Take the Learning Styles Quiz in the back of this book (located in Battle Resources: C).

2. Fill out the "See It, Say It, Do It" section of your Plan of Attack in section B of Battle Resources. Be sure to choose the memorization strategies from this chapter that sound like the most fun to you. Also, if there are things in the Active Memorization Ground Rules section that you need to be reminded of, feel free to include that in your chosen list of tactics.

3. Log in to the Warriors of the Word Facebook Group and share a ten second video of you using your favorite Bible memorization tactic, or post a picture of yourself in your favorite memorization spot and share why it is your favorite.

4. Try out some of your chosen memorization tactics for your accountability partner at your next review session. Also, share with your accountability partner where you like to memorize and why.

CHAPTER 7

Sharpen Your Sword

Honing the Skill of Review

I intend always to remind you of these qualities, though you know
them and are established in the truth that you have. I think it right, as
long as I am in this body, to stir you up by way of reminder . . .
And I will make every effort so that after my departure you may be
able at any time to recall these things.
~ 2 Peter 1:12–13, 15

A Sore Throat

"Emily, I don't know if my voice is going to be able to hold up." I croaked to my wife after an eight-hour day of reviewing several different books of the Bible in preparation for one of my upcoming monthly Aaron Is Memorizing The New Testament recitals. On the weekends before my monthly Scripture recitals, my voice began to feel the burn. Most of the time, it required several days of reviewing out loud for six to eight hours straight.

I had started out memorizing the New Testament on great footing and with a lot of momentum. Some of the books in the first month were easy to memorize because I had previously memorized or partially memorized them for Piercing Word productions. In month four, I successfully memorized what I had scheduled to memorize that

AARON

month—*and* I successfully reviewed everything I had memorized in the previous three months.

And then I hit the wall. I knew I had reached my personal capacity. If I wanted to keep up this pace while maintaining everything I had already memorized, I would have to sacrifice more family time or ministry time than I was willing to give up.

I had to make a choice. Should I keep going and try to finish the goal and allow some of the books I had already memorized fall away? Or should I stop and only maintain what I had memorized so far? For me, being a competitive, goal-oriented type of person, there was only one answer. Press on! I decided to neglect the Maintenance Review that was needed to maintain every chapter of every book that I had memorized. This was the first of many disheartening moments to come. But the memorization of the Word was still so sweet to me during this time. I felt God's presence as I daily invited Him into the experience.

Your review process will probably look a little less intense than mine did during that time, but there are some exciting discoveries about the review process that Emily and I made during that time. In this chapter, we will unpack some keys to successful review of memorized Bible passages.

Sticky Notes

I picture the review process like this. During Active Memorization, it feels as though I am posting lots of sticky notes on the wall of my brain, one sticky note for every word of the text I am memorizing. When I return to the wall the next day, I find that some of the sticky notes have fallen to the ground, while others have remained exactly where I placed them. During my review, I apply fresh paste to the sticky notes and return them to their proper locations. The next day when I return, fewer sticky notes have fallen to the ground. I continue to paste and reapply each note until, one day when I return, they have all remained on the wall. However, as the winds of time blow, the once-strong adhesive begins to wear and the sticky notes begin to fall again. If I do not come by the wall every so often to reapply the sticky notes that have fallen, I will have a hard time quoting the entire passage, even if only 20 percent of the sticky notes are missing. This is because as soon as I get to a word or phrase that has fallen away, I stop and cannot proceed. This is an illustration of the necessity of the practice and discipline of review. It is that of a maintenance man, ensuring that all the stickies are properly affixed to the wall. It is also the maintenance man's choice whether or not he will enjoy his job. He can go about it with a complaining spirit or he can sing and dance and smile his way along the wall.

Many people go about *reviewing* what they have memorized in the same boring way they memorized it in the first place—either silently, with a monotone voice, or using the same boring inflection they used the first fifty times they said it. This only makes the brain say, "I don't need to review this. I already know this and said it fifty times yesterday." This makes review even less desirable than Active Memorization for most people. But I have good news! It does not have to be like this.

Review is essential to the memorization process and should not be put in the same category as Active Memorization. It has a completely different rhythm and different rules. By separating review from Active Memorization, you will speed yourself along in your endeavors and be able to clarify your immediate purpose for any given verse or passage you are working on.

There are two main types of review. Let's take a closer look into these two types of review in order to understand the difference between them and know when each can be properly utilized.

Solidification Review

The purpose of Solidification Review is to solidify what you have memorized. Solidification Review should begin the day after your Active Memorization of a verse or passage and continue every day for at least a week. Solidification Review is similar to Active Memorization in that it requires all of your attention and focus. This can be done alone, or it can be done with a friend. However, don't put off Solidification Review simply because you don't have a review partner. When you utilize a review partner, be sure to follow the instructions in the upcoming Triple Win Review section.

Maintenance Review

This is where the blessing of memorizing Scripture begins to dramatically manifest itself. Maintenance Review can be done anywhere and anytime, while doing nearly anything. It can be done while multitasking. You can do Maintenance Review while washing dishes, driving the car, mowing the lawn, cleaning the house, preparing food, getting ready for bed, taking a shower, folding laundry, or any number of other somewhat mindless or repeated physical tasks. It is best done out loud (or in a whisper if you are trying not to disturb others). While Maintenance Review can be done silently, I am personally far too distractable to successfully get through an entire passage that way. But you can feel free to give it a try.

> SWORDPLAY TIP
>
> **Maintenance Review is the only form of review that should be done while multitasking.**

You can write it or sing it or pray it or share it with others. Maintenance Review can be done as often as you like, but if you are like me, you will need to use some structure in order to actually do it often enough that you can maintain the passage.

Maintenance Review should be done for every passage you have actively memorized in the past and want to keep ready on the tip of your tongue.

At first, Maintenance Review should be done at least once a week, starting as soon as you finish Solidification Review of a verse or passage. After you have done weekly Maintenance Review for a couple of months, you may find that you can start going two or three weeks or even a month at a time without doing any Maintenance Review. I would not recommend a Maintenance Review schedule that has intervals longer than a month. If you go longer than a month without doing Maintenance Review, you may find yourself having to do more patchwork on the passage to fill in holes in your memory.

Review Pitfalls

Hemming and hawing

Spending time using filler words like "um" or "oh" when trying to review a passage does not aid one's memorization. Structure your review times so that you minimize hemming and hawing while you try to figure out what your next word or phrase is. Do everything you can to avoid this review pitfall. One easy technique is to allow yourself time to do open-book review. In other words, try to say the passage without looking at the text, but have the Bible open and ready so that you can glance down if you need to. This is not cheating. This is winning. You should be giving yourself a win every time you review the text, not a loss. When we hem and haw, we become discouraged and only affirm the lie in our mind that says, "I can't do this. I might as well just stop."

Expressing frustration versus peaceful pauses

Occasionally, taking a pause to let your brain catch up to your mouth is not a bad thing. The key is to let it be just that: a calm pause. If you fill the space with a scrunched face, clenched fist, self-deprecating, angry words, or other unhelpful and negative verbal or physical action, you are only destroying any confidence you have gained thus far. Trust the memorization process, stay calm, and simply pause.

Avoid interrupting your own thoughts when you blank, with words like "Shoot," "Oh my word, I thought I had it," "I'm sorry," or "I am really bad at this."

> **SWORDPLAY TIP**
>
> **When reviewing, try to stay calm and only make encouraging comments to yourself. Don't allow yourself to become stressed or verbally degrade yourself.**

Fear of blanking

Many people say they can't remember things or memorize. Oftentimes, this is because they are aware of their brain's aptitude to suddenly and completely go blank. This is actually a very normal phenomenon that every person experiences, not just on stage or when trying to recite information. In fact, I blank all the time when I am on stage, but no one would ever know it. Why? Because I don't fear it or allow it to freak me out. I understand that it is a natural human phenomenon. I understand that the same exact thing happens to me when I am at home with my wife and say, "Honey, can you please turn off the . . . the . . . whatever it's called." "Stove?" she replies. "Yes, that!" Both of us laugh at my inability to find the right word in a moment of stress. Did I really forget what the stove was called? No. Was I ever concerned for a moment that I no longer knew the name of my own household appliance? No. I just took a moment to try to let the word come through. Sometimes my wife or a friend can guess where I am headed verbally before I even get there, and other times the conversation has to pause for several seconds so my brain can find the right mental file folder and produce the correct word.

> **SWORDPLAY TIP**
>
> When your mind goes blank during review, simply pause or repeat the last phrase you just said.

Have you ever blanked on a friend's name you have been close to for years? It happens to us, too. Most people think we have some kind of supernatural memory because of the amount of Scripture we memorize in Piercing Word Ministry. We don't. These same exact phenomena happen to us as well. We just choose to respond to them differently. Rather than saying, "Wow. I have a really terrible memory," we choose to laugh lightheartedly at our human imperfections, trust the memorization process, and continue to believe in the truth of God's Word that we are "fearfully and wonderfully made" (see Psalm 139:14).

When your mind goes blank during Scripture memory review, simply pause or repeat the last phrase you just said. Many times, this is all you need to keep right on going. We will unpack this further in the upcoming Triple Win Review section.

Memorizing your mistakes

It is easy to unknowingly spend time memorizing our mistakes rather than finding creative ways to fix our mistakes and properly connect the thoughts together. We memorize our mistakes when we *tolerate* them as we review rather than *purposing* to smooth them over and fix them. In the Triple Win Review section, we will outline the most effective way to tackle your mistakes and fix them rather than reinforce them.

> **SWORDPLAY TIP**
>
> As you review, make sure to fix your mistakes rather than reinforcing them.

Triple Win Review

The Triple Win Review is a simple and effective way to review Scripture with a review partner. This process will help you avoid all the pitfalls mentioned above.

The three wins described below should be done in immediate succession. This Triple Win Review works best when it is done exactly as prescribed below in one continuous review session.

Win #1

Quote the passage on your own using an open-book review style. This is your first time reviewing the passage today. Let's make it a good one. This may feel like a "cheater" version of review, but that is what we want. We want it to feel good with no mistakes in it. Don't allow yourself to hem or haw or struggle for any words or phrases. You should quote with the Bible open. Allow your eyes to drop and glance at the next word or phrase whenever needed. Be sure to do this review *out loud, as always*. And be sure *not* to do this in front of your review partner. Tell him or her to grab some coffee or something before you get started. Then go into a separate room to do your open-book review first.

Win #2

Quote the passage to your review partner while he or she marks your mistakes. Give the following instructions to your review partner before you begin quoting.

- "Please do not stop me or correct me while I review." This is important because you want to operate from the right side of your brain, the creative side, while you quote with expression for your friend. This will help you maintain momentum and confidence, even if you need to fudge a word or two or slightly paraphrase to keep going. This will not only build your confidence but also help you continue to string together the big picture thoughts first, before critiquing the individual words. Remember: memorize the thoughts first and then the words will come.

- "Give me the next word or phrase *only* when I call for 'line.'"

(This is a common theatre practice when someone forgets a line during rehearsal. The actor simply says "line," and the stage manager, who is looking at the script, will read the actor's next phrase as a prompt. This is a valuable and concise way to keep things flowing. We highly recommend using the word "line" rather than saying, "Can you give me the next few words, please?" It saves so much time and does not derail your focus as much.

- You will need to tell your review partner to let you pause if need be. It is *your* decision when you need a line from your review partner. If he or she starts to give it to you when you pause, simply say, "Please don't give it to me until I call for a line."

- "Mark all my mistakes in pencil." We have created a suggested key that has worked well for us, but feel free to make your own key. The point is that your mistakes are clearly recorded so you can easily fix them after you quote through the passage. If you are not comfortable with pencil markings in your Bible, go to Biblegateway.com and print out the passage in the version you are memorizing. You will find our suggested Mark Up Review Key on the next page.

See the Review Partner Mark Up Key in section E of Battle Resources for a version of these markings that you can easily photocopy and hand to your review partner.

Fixing time

Now ask your review partner to get another cup of coffee while you take a few minutes to use the left side of your brain—the logical and logistics side—to troubleshoot and fix your mistakes one by one. Take a look at the marks your review partner made and review the correct wording or phrasing of your trouble spots *out loud*. The great thing about doing it like this is that you literally only have to focus on the parts that are broken. This is not the time to read or quote the entire passage again. You are only fixing any broken pieces.

Even as you are in fixing mode, however, you will use your left side of the brain to figure out a creative solution. And then you will use your right side of the brain to implement the creativity and patch up the memorization hole with your creative choice. (See the section in chapter 9 about tying together two side-by-side verses that do not seem to go together at all.)

Paraphrased 〜〜〜

Example: We are ambassadors for Christ
           〜〜〜〜〜〜〜〜〜〜

Omitted ⬭

Example: We are ambassadors (for Christ)

Inserted Word/Phrase ^

                                           Jesus

Example: We are ambassadors for ⌄Christ

Swapped Words/Phrases ↰ ↱

Example: We are ambassadors for Christ

Paused ∗

Example: We are ∗ambassadors for Christ

Prompted /

Example: We are ambassadors/for Christ

Needs Work ▭

Example: | We are ambassadors for Christ |

After you are done fixing, grab your review partner and tell him or her you are ready for round two.

Win #3

Quote the passage again for your review partner while he or she marks your mistakes and *erases your corrected mistakes.* If you have done your left-brain fixing well, this will be an encouraging run. When you finish and your review partner hands the Bible or printout back to you, you may find that most of your mistakes have been corrected. This third and final win will greatly boost your confidence moving forward and convince your mind and your heart that you do indeed have the passage memorized.

Well, there you have it. The Triple Win Review process. We hope you will use it often, especially for Maintenance Review. But it can also be used for Solidification Review if desired. Remember: reviewing consistently is the biggest key to good memorization retention. So be sure to schedule your review times with your review partner during your memorization planning stage, *before* you start memorizing.

Your progress through the memorization process

- ☑ Know Why
- Know How
  - ☑ Plan It
  - ☑ Understand It
  - ☑ See It, Say It, Do It
  - ☑ **REVIEW IT**
  - ☐ Apply It
  - (Repeat)

1. Name one new thing about the review process that you learned from this chapter and are excited to incorporate.

   _____

   _____

2. Fill out the "Review It" section of your Plan of Attack in Battle Resources: section B.

3. Have your review partner take a video of you reciting your passage. Then log in to the Warriors of the Word Facebook Group and post your video as an encouragement to the group! If you don't have Facebook, ask the Holy Spirit who in your life could use the Scriptural encouragement and send your video to that person or group of people.

CHAPTER 8

Boots on the Ground

Real-Life Application

Be doers of the word, and not hearers only, deceiving yourselves.
For if anyone is a hearer of the word and not a doer,
he is like a man who looks intently at his natural face in a mirror.
For he looks at himself and goes away and at once forgets
what he was like. But the one who looks into the perfect law,
the law of liberty, and perseveres, being no hearer who forgets but
a doer who acts, he will be blessed in his doing.~ James 1:22–25

Good soldiers don't remain in boot camp forever. After successfully completing boot camp training, a soldier naturally moves on to the battlefield. The same applies in the spiritual realm. You must enter the spiritual battlefield and apply the truths from God's Word that you have trained into your mind and heart. You can do this in three simple ways: *live it, pray it, share it.*

How are you going to apply the Word you have memorized and let it affect every battle of your day? How are you going to purpose to pray the Word over your friends, family, and neighbors? How are you going to share the Word with others?

Perhaps you will begin to see victory over a lifelong sin struggle as you speak God's Word over that issue. Maybe a passage you have

AARON & EMILY

memorized will give you the confidence to step out in faith and follow God in a way that you had been fearful of in the past. Maybe the fruit of the Spirit will become more evident in your life as you meditate on God's truth.

You may begin to pray fewer self-centered prayers as you pray The Lord's Prayer in the mornings. Perhaps you will discover the Holy Spirit's healing energy as you pray God's Word over a friend's broken body. You may find that you finally feel equipped to pray with someone to receive Christ, because you can now articulate the gospel in God's own words.

Perhaps you will start a small accountability group that continues to memorize Scripture together and share it with one another as a regular practice. You may begin to memorize and quote Bible stories as a regular part of the Sunday School class you teach, or even share the gospel from the stage during a church service using the Five-Verse Gospel Presentation.

You might even share memorized Bible passages in unexpected ways. For instance, you might decide to share a memorized verse in a handwritten note to a friend or a loved one. You may include a Scripture passage in an email to a business connection. Perhaps you end up creating a piece of Scripture art that goes on your wall as a constant reminder of God's truth for you and your family.

The possibilities are endless. You will be richly blessed as you live, pray, and share God's Word with those around you. You will experience the transforming power that it holds for you and everyone you interact with.

In this book, you have had glimpses into the lives of many spiritual warriors and how they have wielded Scripture against the enemy's fronts. However, this book is not complete. In fact, I don't think it will ever be complete. It is missing *your* Victory Story. It is missing the testimonies of your family, your friends, the people sitting next to you in church. How has memorizing Scripture impacted *your* life? How is it going to influence the lives of those around you?

It's your time to step out onto the spiritual battlefield with your newly sharpened weapon and watch what the Lord will do. When the Lord grants you victory as you live, pray, and share the Word, write your victory stories. Speak them. Share them. Then turn around and call new recruits into training. Together, let's build a powerful spiritual army to advance the kingdom of God as Warriors of the Word!

Your progress through the memorization process

- ☑ Know Why
- <u>Know How</u>
  - ☑ Plan It
  - ☑ Understand It
  - ☑ See It, Say It, Do It
  - ☑ Review It
  - ☑ **APPLY IT**
  - (Repeat)

1. Is there a time when memorizing God's Word has had a big impact on your life? If so, please journal about your experience here. Then log in to the Warriors of the Word Facebook Group share your Victory Story via a video or a written post.

   _____

   _____

   _____

   _____

   _____

2. Share your Victory Story from the previous question with one or more friends this week. Then ask them if there is a time when they were profoundly touched by memorizing Scripture. Record their answer here.

   _____

   _____

   _____

3. Fill out the "Apply It" section of your Plan of Attack in Battle Resources: B.

4. What are you going to memorize next? Choose your next Bible memorization goal from your Marching Orders and write it in the "Repeat" section of your Plan of Attack in Battle Resources: B. Then invite a new recruit to be your accountability partner and join you by becoming a Warrior of the Word!

CHAPTER 9

Troubleshooting

Common Warrior FAQs

Listen to advice and accept instruction,
that you may gain wisdom in the future. ~ Proverbs 19:20

A Change in Course

As I continued on in my goal to memorize the entire New Testament in 2013, I slowly got further and further behind schedule in my memorization and review plan. The light at the end of the New Testament memorization tunnel was getting further and further away.

After a year of working at this project, it was clear that I needed another six months to one year to complete it. Not only was it a rigorous schedule I had made for myself, but I also had growing demands upon my time as the executive director of a growing full-time Scripture performance ministry. My wife and I were running a discipleship team for high school and college age students. We were touring our professional Scripture performances to many different locations around Lancaster County and beyond. Also, trying to begin a family was heavy on our minds. On top of all this, I had not considered the need for any vacation or travel time when I originally mapped out my memorization plan for the year. Several weeks were lost due to travel and other circumstances. Still, I pressed on, continuing to memorize in 2014.

AARON

After a year and a half, my wife began to struggle with adrenal fatigue. We realized that we needed to slow our pace. We had been running too hard for the last two years; this needed to change. I had another decision to make. Should I continue in the fashion we had for the last two years for the sake of this goal? Or should I listen to my wife and cut something out of our schedule? I decided on the latter. I ended my memorization of the New Testament on July 1st, 2014. At that point, I had successfully memorized and recited before a public audience twenty-five out of twenty-seven books of the New Testament. The only books that I did not complete were Mark and Luke. Since then, I have gotten halfway through memorizing Mark twice. One day, Lord willing, I will complete the task. For now, my greater concern is for the health of my family, the ministry, the many team members that God has entrusted to me, and sharing the truths God has taught me with others.

God broke my pride when I was unable to finish memorizing the New Testament according to my goals. I believe he did this to keep me humble before him and before you. Also, he taught me that the life we have in him is not about heroism. It's about unity. We can do so much more together than we can do alone. That is another reason I am not in a hurry to finish the project. Not only do I not need my pride to be boosted but, more importantly, my efforts need to be focused on unity and building up the body of Christ, not trying to be the hero.

As you set out to memorize God's Word, you will come up against hurdles. You will have questions and need encouragement. We have written this chapter to both empathize with these things and hopefully provide some answers to some commonly asked questions. I had many struggles in my attempt to memorize the New Testament and God has used those hurdles to make me into who I am today. Don't be discouraged when you come up against a hurdle that you have to troubleshoot. No matter whether or not you complete all of your Bible memorization goals, any time you spend meditating on God's Word will make you a stronger warrior than you were before. Lean into God for wisdom as you train and sharpen your sword. Don't be afraid to make alterations to your Bible memorization plan in order to ensure true spiritual success and stay on the straight and narrow path toward God's glorious Kingdom!

By the grace given to me I say to everyone among you not to think of himself more highly than he ought to think, but to think with sober judgment, each according to the measure of faith that God has assigned. (Romans 12:3)

Him we proclaim, warning everyone and teaching everyone with all wisdom, that we may present everyone mature in Christ. For this I toil, struggling with all his energy that he powerfully works within me. (Colossians 1:28–29)

Which translation is the best to memorize?

You should use whatever translation of the Bible you have. If you have access to multiple translations of the Bible, we recommend memorizing the one that is easiest for you to understand or the one you gravitate toward reading the most. If you are seriously on a search to find out which translation is the most accurate to the Greek and Hebrew text or which translation is the easiest one to read in English, let me point you to some resources to help you select the right translation for you.

Some translations are so rigidly transposed from the Greek and Hebrew text that they are difficult to read or understand in English. It is almost as if the translators had no concern for English sentence structure and syntax whatsoever, but just wanted to preserve as much of the original language as possible. Other translations have been created with such a huge emphasis on English readability that they may lose some of the original intent of the Greek and Hebrew text. And then there is a spectrum of translations that fall anywhere in between these two extremes.

> **SWORDPLAY TIP**
>
> Ask the Holy Spirit to guide you in your translation selection.

The ESV Bible is a true word-for-word (also known as formal equivalent) translation that does not neglect current grammar and rules of the English language. This is why I personally love the ESV version and recommend it for both memorization and study. But there are others who have done good thought-for-thought (also known as functional equivalent) translations and paraphrases of the Bible as well. And depending on what you are looking for—readability or

accuracy—you can determine which translation is the best fit for you. We do recommend doing the bulk of your memorization and study in translations that lean more toward a formal equivalent translation style. The three versions I have personally used for memorization in the past are KJV, NIV (1984), and ESV.

Types of Bible Translations

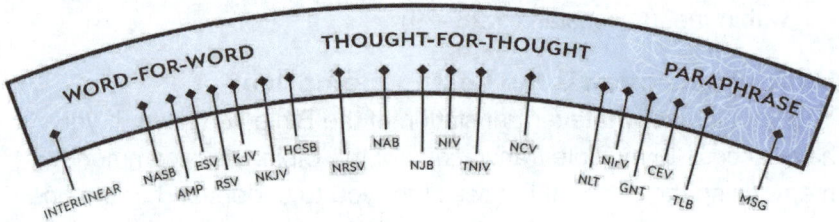

NASB—New American Standard Bible
AMP—Amplified Bible
ESV—English Standard Version
RSV—Revised Standard Version
KJV—King James Version
NKJV—New King James Version
HCSB—Holman Christian Standard Bible
NRSV—New Revised Standard Version
NAB—New American Bible
NJB—New Jerusalem Bible
NIV—New International Version
TNIV—Today's New International Version
NCV—New Century Version
NLT—New Living Translation
NIrV—New International Reader's Version
GNT—Good News Translation (also, Good News Bible)
CEV—Contemporary English Version
TLB—The Living Bible
MSG—The Message

A note to our KJV-only friends. For those of you who hold to a KJV-only stance, I want to let you know that we love you all very much, and we hope that we have not offended you by anything we have said in this book. If we have, we ask for your forgiveness and for a moment of your time to hear my story. I was (like you) raised in a KJV-only household. However, I did receive an NIV Bible (1984 version) as a teenager and really loved it.

In college, I decided I would settle the matter once and for all of which translation was the best by doing some personal research. I went to the library and checked out books that supported both sides of the argument: KJV-only books and books that support other translations. Those are pretty much the only books I could find on Bible translations—those that supported KJV only and those that did not—which I found interesting.

As I began to read the arguments on both sides and looked into the potential pitfalls and consequences of the various translations mentioned, I realized something. None of the complaints on either side had anything to do with the centrality of the gospel. They were nit-picking flaws in the other translation that, if overlooked, would have zero effect on the power of the gospel to transform the lives of those who read it. So I found their arguments to be meaningless controversies, which is exactly what Paul tells us to avoid in the books of Timothy and Titus:

> Have nothing to do with foolish, ignorant controversies; you know that they breed quarrels. And the Lord's servant must not be quarrelsome but kind to everyone, able to teach, patiently enduring evil, correcting his opponents with gentleness. God may perhaps grant them repentance leading to a knowledge of the truth, and they may come to their senses and escape from the snare of the devil, after being captured by him to do his will. (2 Timothy 2:23–26)

> The saying is trustworthy, and I want you to insist on these things, so that those who have believed in God may be careful to devote themselves to good works. These things are excellent and profitable for people. But avoid foolish controversies, genealogies, dissensions, and quarrels about the law, for they are unprofitable and worthless. As for a person who stirs up division, after warning him once and then twice, have nothing more to do with him, knowing that such a person is warped and sinful; he is self-condemned. (Titus 3:8–11)

I returned the books to the library. I could not even finish them. It was just a bunch of mud-slinging and hateful words, which are completely out of place among brothers and sisters in Christ. The conclusion I came to was that I could not indulge the arguments of either side, nor could I take those arguments and build my entire Christian belief system on them. They are unstable ground. I can only build my faith on the person and work of Jesus Christ, the One who died for our sins and was raised for our justification. On this Rock I place my faith, not in some specific translation crafted by man.

In that moment, I made the Lord, not the King James Bible, the true cornerstone of my faith, and my faith became more certain than ever. Just to be clear, I *love* the KJV Bible. I always have and I always will. But it is not the KJV Bible that saved me from my sins and made me righteous before God. It is Jesus who has done this. Regardless of the intent of the various translators of the English translations of the Bible over the years, all of them preach Jesus Christ, crucified and raised on the third day. So I say along with Paul in Philippians:

> Some indeed preach Christ from envy and rivalry, but others from good will . . . *What then? Only that in every way, whether in pretense or in truth, Christ is proclaimed, and in that I rejoice.* (Philippians 1:15, 18, emphasis added)

I will leave you with these words from Paul's letter to the Romans:

> As for the one who is weak in faith, welcome him, but not to quarrel over opinions . . . Who are you to pass judgment on the servant of another? It is before his own master that he stands or falls. And he will be upheld, for the Lord is able to make him stand. One person esteems one day as better than another, while another esteems all days alike. Each one should be fully convinced in his own mind . . . Therefore let us not pass judgment on one another any longer, but rather decide never to put a stumbling block or hindrance in the way of a brother . . . For the kingdom of God is not a matter of eating and drinking but of righteousness and peace and joy in the Holy Spirit. Whoever thus serves Christ is acceptable to God and approved by men. So then let us pursue what makes for peace and for mutual upbuilding. Do not, for the sake of food, destroy the work of God. Everything is indeed clean, but it is wrong for anyone to make another stumble by what he eats. It is good not to eat meat or drink wine or do anything that causes your brother to

stumble. The faith that you have, keep between yourself and God. Blessed is the one who has no reason to pass judgment on himself for what he approves . . . For whatever does not proceed from faith is sin. (Romans 14:1, 4–5, 13, 17–23)

Ask the Holy Spirit to guide you in your translation selection. After you have done your research and taken it to the Lord, use whatever translation(s) you feel at peace using. At the same time, let us not pass judgment on one another for our choice of translation. It is before our own Master that we stand or fall. Let us not, for the sake of translation, destroy the work of God.

Should I memorize the verse references?

Verse references can be very difficult to memorize and sometimes unnecessary to memorize. At Piercing Word, we highly recommend memorizing entire passages or chapters rather than individual verses most of the time. If you memorize an entire chapter, the only reference you need to memorize is the book name and chapter number. It can be detrimental and distracting from your understanding of the entire passage if you attempt to memorize the individual verse numbers for each verse in the chapter you are memorizing. Because of this, we do not recommend memorizing verse numbers when memorizing an entire chapter of the Bible.

However, if you are memorizing a single verse or even two or three verses in a row, you should memorize the book name, chapter number, and verse number(s) along with it. You need to know where to find the verse again in the future. Knowing the reference to a single verse is imperative, whether you need to review the verse you have memorized, show the verse to a friend, or re-read the surrounding context.

The reason verse references are difficult to memorize is because the numbers mean almost nothing to us in relation to one another. In other words, there is not an inherent connecting thought process or storyline that helps our minds tie the numbers and concepts together naturally. However, there are multiple memorization systems that can help with memorizing numbers. Perhaps the most widely popular and easily learned is called the Major System. The Major System is a type of Phonetic Number System that is used to aid in memorizing numbers and playing cards. The premise of this system is that it is much easier to memorize images and words than numbers. The system enables you to turn any grouping of numbers into consonant sounds and then into words by adding vowels. These words can become living images that can be stored in a memory palace in our minds. If you would like to learn more about how to use the simple and effective Major System, simply type "The Major System" or "The Major Memory System" into your internet search bar.

How can I memorize lists?

Lists can at times feel difficult to memorize, but they don't have to be if you have a few tricks up your sleeve.

1. Make an acronym out of the first letter of each word in the list. See if it makes a funny "word" you can use to help jog your memory (like the example of "MAD SEL" in chapter 6).

2. Make a bizarre and memorable sentence using the first letter of each word in the list. For example, we often do this with Paul's epistles to the Galatians, Ephesians, Philippians, and Colossians. People have come up with several funny sentences to remember this order: "*Go Eat Pop Corn*"; "*Gentiles Eat Pork Chops*"; "*General Electric Power Company*."

3. Utilize hand motions. Make up a hand motion for each item in the list. Try to find hand motions that flow easily into each other, so that when you finish one hand motion, your brain will remember what comes next because your hands naturally want to go there.

4. Make a bizarre mental picture including all the items in the list. Make a bizarre story out of it; it doesn't have to have anything to do with what the Scripture is actually saying. The crazier it is, the more it sticks in your mind!

5. Use bizarre word or picture associations (as discussed in chapter 6 on learning styles).

Why is this passage harder than the last one?

There are many reasons this could be happening to you. The first place to check is your memorization journal. Did you do something differently during today's memorization session than you did in the previous one? If so, take note of it. Did you change memorization locations, techniques, body positions? Did you have more distractions, either external or internal?

If all of these elements are the same, perhaps the passage has a biblical concept that you have not fully grasped. Take time to paraphrase it in your own words to ensure you understand it fully.

If you understand the passage and did not change your memorization methods, the most likely possibility is that this passage is literally harder to memorize than the last one. It could be that the passage you are memorizing has a list of difficult Bible names in it or sections that don't seem to flow together as well in English.

Each person is somewhat different regarding what types of passages they find harder or easier. But generally speaking, the easiest passages to memorize are usually story narratives, such as are found in the Gospels (Matthew, Mark, Luke, and John), Old Testament stories, and certain Psalms. Other passages range in difficulty level. Emily says that Hebrews contained some of the hardest passages she ever memorized simply because some of the concepts are culturally foreign and can be difficult to understand at first glance.

The passages that were the most difficult for me when memorizing the New Testament were the passages that were similar to passages found elsewhere in the Bible. I would often get to these similar passages and get derailed from the intended quotation.

What if I neglect Maintenance Review for a long time and can't remember what I memorized?

This happens to the best of us. Sometimes life gets busy and unpredictable and we neglect to follow through on the best of intentions. When this happens, the "bad news" is that you will have to re-memorize the passage and it will take extra time, effort, and work. However, rememorizing is not just work. The good news is when you re-memorize a passage, you get to meditate again on its truths and rediscover the richness in its depths! Plus, Re-memorization happens twice as fast as regular Active Memorization. Even though it can be disheartening to watch a passage of Scripture fall away from memory, be encouraged with the fact that, most of the time, *it has not completely fallen away.* As you dive back into memorizing the passage again, your brain will quickly remember the work it did months or years ago when you first memorized it. You will have that passage up and running again in no time!

Do I have to memorize the Bible word for word?

Some Bible memorization methodologies entail only a solid thought-for-thought recall. In chapter 3, I told a story of Larry Dinkins, the missionary to Thailand, who paid me a visit and told me about Simply The Story's global discipleship program.[7]

During that meeting, Larry described to me the basic memorization methodology used by Simply The Story. Once an Optimum Bible Story is selected (we explain Optimum Bible Stories in greater detail in chapter 3), you can start thought-for-thought absorption by standing up and reading the passage out loud one time. Then lay the Bible down and repeat the entire story out loud as best as you can remember it without looking at all. While you do this, be sure to picture the story in your mind and use your body to express the actions within the story. Once you finish telling the Bible story once through in your own words, then pick up the Bible and read it again out loud. Put the Bible down and try to tell the story again without looking at all. Then pick up the Bible again and check to see if you missed any important details. Put the Bible down and try to tell the story again. Continue this process until you are close to getting the story content accurate. Remember, it's okay if you use synonyms for certain words or phrases or a proper name instead of a pronoun. You should give yourself an A+ if all the details of the story remain intact. The goal is to tell the story with content accuracy but tell it naturally in your own words.

In using this technique, Larry has memorized many Bible stories and can tell them accurately with little review necessary. He has discovered the beauty of memorizing entire passages of Scripture. In this manner, he has been able to tuck many multiverse passages into his heart pocket much more efficiently and lastingly than the traditional individual verse and reference memorization approach that most American Christians associate with Bible memory.

We believe this is a valid and effective Bible memorization method that has been used globally by Simply The Story. They successfully and continually disciple people across the world on how to remember, share, and discuss Bible stories accurately. Their technique affirms an accurate telling of each Bible story but avoids the barrier of trying to tell it in a rote word-for-word manner which proves to be a stumbling block for many believers. They have discovered and capitalized on the most important thing about Bible memory—it's about stringing the correct thoughts together, not the correct words. This truth is evidenced by the 450 English Bible translations alone! Clearly, if you can say something 450 different ways in order to get the same message across, the importance lies in the thoughts, not the words. (As discussed earlier in this chapter, not all translations are created equal. See the above section for more of our thoughts on translations.)

In the Piercing Word Bible Memorization Process, we recommend and teach people to go one step further than thought-for-thought memorization into word-for-word memorization. But before you can successfully memorize something word for word, you must first memorize and internalize it thought for thought.

One of the biggest reasons we recommend memorizing the Bible word for word is because you can be more pointed with the sword of truth in a moment of need. Most good lies are 99 percent truth. So, if you know the Bible word for word, it will be much more difficult for you to be deceived by the lies of the enemy. Also, it will greatly increase your confidence in sharing truth with others.

In fact, in talking with Larry, he agreed with this sentiment and said that, although memorizing individual Bible verses word for word is more difficult than absorbing Bible stories, he highly encourages every disciple of Christ to do so. He said there are many times when an individual verse will be needed as you witness, counsel, disciple, preach, or meditate on God's Word.

The Simply The Story method of absorbing Bible stories is effective and worth trying, especially if you find yourself getting hung up on individual words. You may find great success in telling the Bible story accurately rather than reciting it word for word. This is a great method to help free you from the legalism of trying to recite word for word too early in your memorization process.

Another benefit of this Bible story absorption method is that it requires less review than word-for-word memorization. Don't let the legalism or difficulty of word-for-word memorization stop you from internalizing God's Word. You can definitely use thought-for-thought memorization and successfully hide God's Word in your heart!

These two side-by-side verses do not go together at all! How am I supposed to string them together in my memory? It feels like a sudden change in topic!

EMILY

This is a great question, and there are a number of places in the Bible where this happens. Here, I would employ the bizarre visual picture association method if at all possible. Or if not that, then hand motions that flow well from one verse to the next. Let me give you an example of a bizarre visual picture association with Psalm 139:17–24.

> How precious to me are your thoughts, O God!
>> How vast is the sum of them!
> If I would count them, they are more than the sand.
>> I awake, and I am still with you.
> Oh that you would slay the wicked, O God!
>> O men of blood, depart from me!
> They speak against you with malicious intent;
>> your enemies take your name in vain.
> Do I not hate those who hate you, O Lord?
>> And do I not loathe those who rise up against you?
> I hate them with complete hatred;
>> I count them my enemies.
> Search me, O God, and know my heart!
>> Try me and know my thoughts!
> And see if there be any grievous way in me,
>> and lead me in the way everlasting!

This beautiful psalm is one of my favorites, but the section about the wicked always felt like a jarring subject change to me. These kinds of subject changes in passages often make a *lot* more sense when you study the passage in context. But even then, they can be hard for our brains to grasp if we do not find a creative way to associate them. Let's explore how we can creatively connect these sections of Psalm 139 in our brain.

> How precious to me are your thoughts, O God!
>> How vast is the sum of them!
> If I would count them, they are more than the sand.

Picture yourself lying on the sand at the beach, counting God's thoughts (instead of sheep) to help you fall asleep.

> I awake, and I am still with you.
> Oh that you would slay the wicked, O God!
>> O men of blood, depart from me!
> They speak against you with malicious intent;
>> your enemies take your name in vain.
> Do I not hate those who hate you, O Lord?
>> And do I not loathe those who rise up against you?
> I hate them with complete hatred;
>> I count them my enemies.

While you are sleeping, you have a bad dream. You wake with a start, jumping to your feet and brandishing an invisible sword to slay your enemies.

> Search me, O God, and know my heart!
>> Try me and know my thoughts!
> And see if there be any grievous way in me,
>> and lead me in the way everlasting!

You are suddenly wrought with conviction from the Lord. You throw down your sword and fall to your knees, praying to the Lord to search your heart and make it clean.

Remember, this does not take the place of studying the passage and understanding why the subject change is there. This is a technique for helping your brain to string together two things it sees as unlike items. Don't forget, the more bizarre your picture association, the better! If it makes you laugh, you'll remember it!

How can I learn to memorize things other than the Bible?

Many of the Bible memorization tactics in this book can be applied to any type of information you would like to memorize. Keeping the skill of memorization sharp and ready will help you in nearly every area of life.

At the same time, because the focus of this book is memorizing passages from the Bible, we have not specifically addressed memorization techniques for numbers, addresses, people's names and faces, and other kinds of memorization. Other memorization books that address these subjects more specifically are available. If you desire to expand your knowledge of memorization technique even further, we refer you to these other sources (see section G of Battle Resources).

1. What translation do you intend to use for your memorization?

   _____

   _____

2. Is there a Bible passage you have memorized in the past that you would like to re-memorize? If so, write it here.

   _____

   _____

3. Log in to the Warriors of the Word Facebook Group and ask any questions you currently have or voice any roadblocks you have come up against in your Bible memorization journey. If your memorization is going smoothly, log in and encourage someone else who has recently posted on the page. If you don't have Facebook, feel free to contact us with any questions at www. piercingword.org/contact-us.

Afterword

You may be wondering if I still struggle with all those neurological disorders. Well, I am blessed and excited to share with you that God has completely and totally delivered me from them all!

From age eight to fifteen years, my parents tried me on nearly every neurological medicine on the market, to no avail. At age fifteen, my whole family went on a raw vegan diet which made a dramatic difference in my neurological well-being and behavior.

I continued to limit and be strategic with my diet throughout college, but the rage disorder continued to plague me (though far less often than before). When I was twenty-three, after years of prayer and pleading, the Lord spoke to me and said that would be the year of freedom. Sure enough, that year I had my last rage, and the Lord finally released me entirely from all of my neurological disorders.

So I set up an altar to the Lord—the song "Call to Worship" by Mercy Me. Anytime I am ever tempted to go back to that place of rage, I sing or scream or cry that song to my Father, and he takes the temptation from me. I play that song as an altar of remembrance for what the Lord has done for me. When I come to that altar, I continually thank God for delivering me. He took me from being a boy full of anger and rage to a man of peace. It is God who has made me who I am today.

AARON

The Arsenal

1. ABC Verses for Kids of All Ages
2. Scripture Song Resources
3. Life Verses
4. Gospel Verses
5. Build Your Own Five-Verse Gospel Presentation
6. Five-Minute Gospel Presentation Word for Word from the ESV Bible
7. Temptation Fighters and Fear Fighters
8. Prayers
9. Prophecy
10. Tellable Bible Stories
11. Church Challenge Chart

ABC Verses for Kids of All Ages

All verses are in ESV unless otherwise noted. The second half of some verses have been italicized. This italicized portion is optional depending on whether you would like to memorize a shorter version of the passage or a longer version.

A—**A**ll have sinned and fall short of the glory of God. (Romans 3:23)

B—**B**elieve in the Lord Jesus and you will be saved. (Acts 16:31)

C—**C**ount it all joy, *my brothers, when you meet trials of various kinds.* (James 1:2)

D—**D**o everything without complaining and arguing. (Philippians 2:14 NLT)

E—**E**ven a child makes himself known by his acts, by whether his conduct is pure and upright. (Proverbs 20:11)

F—**F**or God so loved the world, that he gave his only Son, that whoever believes in him should not perish but have eternal life. (John 3:16)

G—**G**ive thanks in all circumstances; *for this is the will of God in Christ Jesus for you.* (1 Thessalonians 5:18)

H—**H**onor your father and your mother. (Exodus 20:12)

I—**I** can do all things through Christ who strengthens me. (Philippians 4:13 NKJV)

J—**J**esus Christ is the same yesterday and today and forever. (Hebrews 13:8)

K—**K**eep your tongue from evil and your lips from telling lies. (Psalm 34:13 NIV)

L—Love the Lord your God with all your heart and with all your soul and with all your might. (Deuteronomy 6:5)

M—My grace is sufficient for you, *for my power is made perfect in weakness.* (2 Corinthians 12:9)

N—No one born of God makes a practice of sinning. (1 John 3:9)

O—Oh, taste and see that the Lord is good! (Psalm 34:8)

P—Pray without ceasing. (1 Thessalonians 5:17)

Q—In Quietness and in trust shall be your strength. (Isaiah 30:15)

R—Rejoice in the Lord always; *again I will say, rejoice.* (Philippians 4:4)

S—Seek first the kingdom of God and his righteousness, and all these things will be added to you. (Matthew 6:33)

T—Take care, and be on your guard against all covetousness, *for one's life does not consist in the abundance of his possessions.* (Luke 12:15)

U—Unto you is born this day in the city of David a Savior, *who is Christ the Lord.* (Luke 2:11)

V—Vanity of vanities, says the Preacher; *all is vanity.* (Ecclesiastes 12:8)

W—Whatever you do, work heartily, as for the Lord and not for men. (Colossians 3:23)

X—EXalt the LORD our God; *worship at his footstool! Holy is he!* (Psalm 99:5)

Y—You shall love your neighbor as yourself. (Galatians 5:14)

Z—Be Zealous and repent. (Revelation 3:19)

Scripture Song Resources

Steve Green - Hide 'Em in Your Heart Scripture Memory Songs

These songs are *amazingly* well done, catchy, and a blessing to have playing in your household at all times. Parents can enjoy listening and being encouraged by them just as much as the children! You can purchase *Hide 'Em In Your Heart Volumes 1 & 2* and *Hide 'Em In Your Heart Praise and Worship* at https://stevegreenministries.org/store.

Seeds Family Worship

These albums are made by an awesome family that loves helping other families plant the "seeds" of God's Word in their hearts! Geared toward children, *Seeds Family Worship* is a collection of word-for-word Scripture songs on either CD or DVD, categorized according to different biblical themes. On the DVDs, each song has fun and engaging video footage and one of their children excitedly doing hand motions. This is a great way to get your kids on their feet and physically engaged in memorizing Scripture. Doing hand motions as you sing Scripture songs utilizes multiple learning style tactics at once, and will have you learning Scripture in no time! Purchase them at https://www.seedsfamilyworship.com/store/music/.

NIV Kids Club

Stan Blair, a professional opera singer with a heart for kids and for God's Word, created an organization called NIV Kids Club. The tagline for his ministry is "Singing the Bible and having fun." This could not be more true! Ideal for preschool and elementary ages,

NIV Kids Club is a collection of DVDs overflowing with word-for-word Scripture songs sung by a bunch of happy kids having a blast learning the Bible, led by the goofy Mr. Stan. Our preschool kiddos find these DVDs fun and engaging—a huge win! Purchase them at http://nivkids.com/purchase.shtml.

The Bible Song

The Bible Song is a project by Word For Word Ministries, Inc. David Newquist is the founder of this ministry, and he has set the entire New Testament to music. He has plans to do the same with the Old Testament as well. They have already produced the first chapter of each New Testament book and are in the process of making all of them available online. This is an incredible and well-done resource! People are using these Scripture songs to memorize entire chapters of the Bible. Word For Word Ministries is also looking for groups to sponsor the composition and production of more chapters. David is also seeking composers and music artists to assist in completing the work. You will definitely want to check this out. https://www.biblesong.com.

Piercing Word

We have several original cast recordings available from our fully Scripture musicals. These songs have been taken word for word from the ESV Bible and have been composed in a musical theatre style. You can download these songs from our website at https://piercingword.org/downloads.

Mark Altrogge

This pastor from Indiana, Pennsylvania, originally began putting word-for-word Scripture to music to aid himself and his family in Scripture memorization. Later, he decided to make his hard work available to everyone and now has ten albums full of word-for-word Scripture songs. These songs are well done and are a wonderful memorization tool for all ages. Find them at http://www.forevergratefulmusic.com/.

Scripture Memory Fellowship

Scripture Memory Fellowship has number of Scripture song albums that complement their various Bible memorization resources, such as their SwordGrip series. Be sure to put these Scripture songs to good use. You can find them at https://Scripturememory.com/products-resources/other-products/Scripture-songs.

Hidden In My Heart Scripture Lullabies

These stunningly beautiful songs are soothing for every age and have truly helped to change the atmosphere in our home and put our focus back on Jesus and the truth of his Word during times of stress, fear, or pain. The one disclaimer I will give on this set is that many of the songs are not word-for-word Scripture songs, but instead, Scripture-based songs, so don't assume that every song you memorize from this set is an exact verse. The scriptural truths within these songs are striking and comforting, and the music is beautifully tranquil. Purchase *Hidden In My Heart: A Lullaby Journey Through Scripture Volumes 1 & 2*, and *Volume 3, Hidden In My Heart: A Lullaby Journey Through the Life of Jesus* at https://Scripture-lullabies.com/shop#hidden-in-my-heart.

Shane and Shane

Shane Barnard and Shane Everett are an acoustic duo with incredible vocal harmonies and biblical truths in their music. Their music has been a favorite go-to of ours for years. Their heart for worship and their love for God's Word shine through every song. Many of their songs and albums are inspired by Scripture, but they also have specific albums and songs that are word-for-word Scripture. Check out their many albums at https://shaneandshane.shop/product-category/music/page/1.

Life Verse Examples

Feel free to choose one of the following verses to memorize and apply as your personal life verse , or select your own. Remember, a life verse should continually recenter and refocus you on Christ and remind you of your identity in him.

> I have been crucified with Christ. It is no longer I who live, but Christ who lives in me. And the life I now live in the flesh I live by faith in the Son of God, who loved me and gave himself for me. (Galatians 2:20)

> Indeed, I count everything as loss because of the surpassing worth of knowing Christ Jesus my Lord. For his sake I have suffered the loss of all things and count them as rubbish, in order that I may gain Christ. (Philippians 3:8; (Aaron's life verse)

> Whatever you do, work at it with all your heart, as working for the Lord, not for human masters, since you know that you will receive an inheritance from the Lord as a reward. It is the Lord Christ you are serving. (Colossians 3:23–24)

> And whatever you do, in word or deed, do everything in the name of the Lord Jesus, giving thanks to God the Father through him. (Colossians 3:17)

> Therefore, if anyone is in Christ, he is a new creation. The old has passed away; behold, the new has come. (2 Corinthians 5:17)

And he [Jesus] said to all, "If anyone would come after me, let him deny himself and take up his cross daily and follow me. For whoever would save his life will lose it, but whoever loses his life for my sake will save it. For what does it profit a man if he gains the whole world and loses or forfeits himself?" (Luke 9:23–25)

Trust in the Lord with all your heart, and do not lean on your own understanding. In all your ways acknowledge him, and he will make straight your paths. (Proverbs 3:5–6)

But now thus says the Lord, he who created you, O Jacob, he who formed you, O Israel: 'Fear not, for I have redeemed you. I have called you by name. You are mine." (Isaiah 43:1)

Easy "Grab and Go" Gospel Verses

The Romans Road

Romans 3:23 —For all have sinned and fallen short of the glory of God.

Romans 5:8 —but God shows his love for us in that while we were still sinners, Christ died for us.

Romans 6:23 —For the wages of sin is death, but the free gift of God is eternal life in Christ Jesus our Lord.

Romans 10:9–10 —because, if you confess with your mouth that Jesus is Lord and believe in your heart that God raised him from the dead, you will be saved. For with the heart one believes and is justified, and with the mouth one confesses and is saved.

Romans 10:13 —For everyone who calls on the name of the Lord will be saved.

Build Your Own Five-Verse Gospel Presentation Worksheet

On the following two pages there is an exciting tool for you to build your own short, simple, and understandable gospel presentation that you can use when sharing the gospel with someone individually or when sharing the gospel from the stage for a group. Just go through each of the five sections and select one verse from each section. Then compile them together in a logical order that flows well and makes sense. As long as you use one verse from each section, your gospel presentation should include and concisely present the essential parts of the gospel. It is important to have specific Bible verses memorized when sharing your faith because you are then able to say "God's Word says . . ." rather than "I think the Bible says something like . . .". It grounds your beliefs in concrete truths rather than amorphous feelings or abstract thoughts. The gospel is compelling when it is grounded in biblical truth.

Five Verse Gospel Presentation Worksheet

1. All People Are Sinners

Romans 3:23	For all have sinned and fallen short of the glory of God
James 2:10	For whoever keeps the whole law but fails in one point has become guilty of all of it.
Luke 5:32	I have not come to call the righteous but sinners to repentance.
Isaiah 59:2	but your iniquities have caused a separation between you and your God, and your sins have hidden his face from you so that he does not hear.
1 John 1:8-9	If we say we have no sin, we deceive ourselves, and the truth is not in us. If we confess our sins, he is faithful and just to forgive us our sins and to cleanse us from all unrighteousness.

2. God Is Both Merciful And Just

Psalm 86:15	But you, O Lord, are a God merciful and gracious, slow to anger and abounding in steadfast love and faithfulness.
Acts 17:30	The times of ignorance God overlooked, but now he commands all people everywhere to repent,
Nahum 1:3	The Lord is slow to anger and great in power, and the Lord will by no means clear the guilty.
1 John 4:10	In this is love, not that we have loved God, but that he loved us and sent his son to be the propitiation for our sins.
Numbers 14:18a	The Lord is slow to anger and abounding in steadfast love, forgiving iniquity and transgression, but he will by no means clear the guilty...

3. Jesus Christ Died And Rose Again

Romans 5:8	But God shows his love for us in that while we were still sinners, Christ died for us.
1 Peter 2:24	He himself bore our sins in his body on the tree, that we might die to sin and live to righteousness. By his wounds you have been healed.
1 John 5:12	Whoever has the Son, has life; whoever does not have the Son of God does not have life.
Isaiah 53:6b	...and the LORD has laid on him the iniquity of us all.
John 3:16-17	For God so loved the world, that he gave his only Son, that whoever believes in him should not perish but have eternal life. For God did not send his Son into the world to condemn the world, but in order that the world might be saved through him.

4. Salvation Is A Free Gift

Romans 6:23	For the wages of sin is death, but the free gift of God is eternal life in Christ Jesus our Lord.
Ephesians 2:8-9	For by grace you have been saved through faith. And this is not your own doing; it is the free gift of God, not a result of works, so that no one may boast.
Romans 3:24	We are justified by his grace as a gift, through the redemption that is in Christ Jesus.
1 John 5:11	And this is the testimony, that God gave us eternal life, and this life is in his Son.
Acts 2:38	Repent and be baptized every one of you in the name of Jesus Christ for the forgiveness of your sins, and you will receive the gift of the Holy Spirit.

5. Faith In Christ Alone

Acts 16:31a	...Believe in the Lord Jesus, and you will be saved...
Romans 10:9-10	If you confess with your mouth that Jesus is Lord and believe in your heart that God raised him from the dead, you will be saved. For with the heart one believes and is justified, and with the mouth one confesses and is saved.
Mark 1:15	The time is fulfilled, and the kingdom of God is at hand; repent and believe in the gospel.
Acts 4:12	And there is salvation in no one else, for there is no other name under heaven given among men by which we must be saved.
John 3:18	Whoever believes in him is not condemned, but whoever does not believe is condemned already, because he has not believed in the name of the only Son of God.

Five Verse Gospel Presentation Worksheet

1. All People Are Sinners

2. God Is Both Merciful And Just

3. Jesus Christ Died And Rose Again

4. Salvation Is A Free Gift

5. Faith In Christ Alone

Five-Minute Gospel Presentation

Word for Word from the ESV
Arranged by Aaron House

This gospel presentation is intended to be memorized and shared in a group or a church setting. It has many verses that are helpful for personal evangelism individually, but this entire presentation is not recommended for one-on-one evangelism.

As an introduction, you can say something like this: "And now, hear the good news of Jesus Christ word for word from the ESV Bible."

(Note: You do *not* need to cite the references when giving the gospel presentation. The references are provided for your own personal reference. Quoting verses aloud without the references makes this gospel presentation fluid and cohesive for those who are listening.)

> Now I would remind you, brothers, of the gospel . . . that Christ died for our sins in accordance with the Scriptures, that he was buried, that he was raised on the third day in accordance with the Scriptures, and that he appeared to Cephas, then to the twelve. Then he appeared to more than five hundred brothers at one time. Then he appeared to James, then to all the apostles. (1 Corinthians 15:1–7)
>
> For God so loved the world, that he gave his only Son, that whoever believes in him should not perish but have eternal life. For God did not send his Son into the world to condemn the world, but in order that the world might be saved through him.

Whoever believes in him is not condemned, but whoever does not believe is condemned already, because he has not believed in the name of the only Son of God. (John 3:16–18)

Whoever does not believe God has made him a liar, because he has not believed in the testimony that God has borne concerning his Son. And this is the testimony, that God gave us eternal life, and this life is in his Son. Whoever has the Son has life; whoever does not have the Son of God does not have life.
(1 John 5:10–12)

Therefore, knowing the fear of the Lord, we persuade others. For the love of Christ controls us, because we have concluded this: that one has died for all, therefore all have died; and he died for all, that those who live might no longer live for themselves but for him who for their sake died and was raised.

Therefore, if anyone is in Christ, he is a new creation. The old has passed away; behold, the new has come. All this is from God, who through Christ reconciled us to himself and gave us the ministry of reconciliation; that is, in Christ God was reconciling the world to himself, not counting their trespasses against them, and entrusting to us the message of reconciliation.

Therefore, we are ambassadors for Christ, God making his appeal through us. We implore you on behalf of Christ, be reconciled to God. For our sake he made him to be sin who knew no sin, so that in him we might become the righteousness of God. (2 Corinthians 5:11–21)

For all have sinned and fall short of the glory of God. (Romans 3:23)

But God shows his love for us in that while we were still sinners, Christ died for us. (Romans 5:8)

For the wages of sin is death, but the free gift of God is eternal life in Christ Jesus our Lord. (Romans 6:23)

It is the gift of God, not a result of works, so that no one may boast. (Ephesians 2:8–9)

If we say we have no sin, we deceive ourselves, and the truth is not in us. If we confess our sins, he is faithful and just to forgive us our sins and to cleanse us from all unrighteousness. (1 John 1:8–9)

Because, if you confess with your mouth that Jesus is Lord and believe in your heart that God raised him from the dead, you will be saved. For with the heart one believes and is justified, and with the mouth one confesses and is saved. For "everyone who calls on the name of the Lord will be saved." (Romans 10:9–13)

After the gospel presentation, give a brief call for people to pray with you to receive Christ. Then pray. You may use the following as a script if you are unsure of what to say.

"You just heard the gospel word for word from the ESV Bible. The word *gospel* means 'good news.' Will you respond to this good news and ask Jesus Christ to forgive your sins and become the Lord of your life? If you have never done that, I invite you to do that right now. If you are ready to turn from your sins and receive all Jesus Christ has for you, pray this prayer with me right now.

"Dear Heavenly Father, thank you for sending your Son, Jesus Christ, to die on the cross and pay the penalty for my sin and for the sin of the whole world. I have done and thought many wrong things in my life. Please forgive me for my sin. Thank you for the promise of the resurrection and for raising Jesus from the dead on the third day. Thank you for giving us your Holy Spirit. I want you to be the Lord of my life. Help me to live every day for you and for your kingdom and not for myself. I love you, Lord Jesus. Amen."

Temptation Fighter and Fear Fighter Verse Examples

LUST

Below is a list of seven great passages that Aaron memorized to combat lust. We have also found it helpful to memorize verses that are specifically focused on the Lord and how he satisfies our every need. When we focus on the Lord, Satan loses power. If you focus too much on battling the sin, sometimes you just end up thinking about the sin even more, which is not beneficial. If you want to go deeper than these listed here, we recommend memorizing all of 1 Corinthians 6:9–20, as Aaron did. All of these passages are great for a quick stab of truth at the enemy in a time of temptation.

Job 31:1

1 Corinthians 6:18–20

Colossians 3:5–6

Romans 8:1

1 Corinthians 6:13

1 Corinthians 10:12–13

Hebrews 12:4

FEAR

We compiled this list during a time when Emily was battling fear. These are six great passages to memorize in order to combat the fear tactics that Satan so often uses to derail our faith in Christ.

2 Timothy 1:6–7

1 John 4:18

Psalm 34:7

Romans 8:15

Psalm 34:4

Proverbs 10:24

On the next page, record your own fighter verses.

Now it's your turn! Write a current fear or temptation you face. Then search for and find five to seven verses that speak directly to that issue. Write them below.

My Current Temptation or Fear:_____

Fighter Verse #1

_____

Fighter Verse #2

_____

Fighter Verse #3

_____

Fighter Verse #4

_____

Fighter Verse #5

_____

Fighter Verse #6

_____

Fighter Verse #7

_____

Stumped?

Order Navigator's *Topical Memory System: Life Issues* edition or the original *Navigators Topical Memory System*. These Bible verse memory card sets come with several different Bible translations and cover many different common life struggles. The cool thing is each life issue has six memory cards addressing that topic, which makes it the perfect complement for your Bible Memorization Marching Orders!

THE ARSENAL: 8
Prayers in the Bible

This is a collection of amazing prayers in the Bible for you to be encouraged by and consider memorizing to utilize in your own prayer life. This is not an exhaustive list, so feel free to share with us any other prayers in the Bible that you have been encouraged by.

Numbers 6:24–26	Prayer of Blessing
1 Chronicles 4:10	The Prayer of Jabez
Nehemiah 1:4–11	Prayer for Forgiveness and Favor
Psalm 6	Prayer for Mercy and Healing
Psalm 23	The Lord is My Shepherd
Psalm 27:7–14	Prayer for God's Presence
Psalm 51	Prayer of Confession
Psalm 55	Casting the Burden of Betrayal on the Lord
Psalm 77	Prayer for a Day of Trouble
Psalm 84	Prayer of Longing for the Courts of the Lord
Psalm 86	Prayer for a Day of Trouble 2
Psalm 104	Praise for God's Majesty and Awesome Deeds
Psalm 119:4–40	Prayer of Commitment to God's Word

Psalm 139	Search Me, O God, and Know My Heart
Psalm 143	My Soul Thirsts for God
Psalm 144	Blessing for Those whose God is the Lord
Psalm 145	Prayer of Praise
Daniel 9:3–19	Prayer of Personal and Corporate Confession
Matthew 6:9–13	The Lord's Prayer
Ephesians 1:16–21	Prayer for Wisdom and Revelation
Ephesians 3:14–21	Prayer for Strength and Grounding in Love
Philippians 1:9–11	Prayer for Discernment and Spiritual Fruit
Philippians 4:19–20	Prayer for Needs to be Met
Colossians 1:9–14	Prayer for the Knowledge of God's Will and Endurance
1 Thessalonians 3:11–13	Prayer for Loved Ones Who Are Far Away
2 Thessalonians 1:11–12	Prayer for Empowerment for One's Calling

THE ARSENAL: 9
End Times Prophecy Passages

This is a collection of end times prophecies in the Bible for you to read and to consider memorizing to help you be watchful for our Lord's coming. This is not an exhaustive list, so feel free to share with us any other end times prophecies in the Bible that you have discovered.

Old Testament
Isaiah 13, 14, 24, 25, 26, 27, 33, 34, 51, 65
Ezekiel 37–48
Daniel 7–12
Joel
Amos 9
Zephaniah 1:14–18; 3:8–20
Haggai 2:1–9
Zechariah 11–14
Malachi 4:1–5

New Testament
Matthew 24–25
Mark 13
Luke 12:35–56
Luke 21:5–36
1 Thessalonians 5:1–11
2 Thessalonians 1:5–12
2 Thessalonians 2:1–12
2 Peter 3
Jude 1:17–25
Revelation

110 Tellable Bible Stories

Compiled by Paul Koehler
author of *Telling God's Stories with Power*

A note from Paul Koehler: These exciting and effective stories range from Genesis to Acts. Seventy-five of the stories are less than five hundred words and can be told in five minutes or less. Twenty stories are under two hundred words. Only six are over one thousand words. The stories are sorted by the order they appear in the Bible. As you progress, you may want to tell some of the stories in sequential order, for instance stories about Bible characters like Moses, Daniel, or Paul. This is not a comprehensive list. Many stories have been left out because they are longer or more difficult to learn. The twenty stories about Jesus's birth and crucifixion are not included but are wonderful stories to learn. So if you don't see your favorite Bible story here, just add it to your list. Most importantly, pick a story and get started. Learn the story, practice it, and then make a plan to tell it to someone.

Garden of Eden	Genesis 2:5-25	510 words
How Evil Came to the World	Genesis 3:1-24	700 words
Cain and Abel	Genesis 4:1-12,16-17, 25-26	350 words
Tower of Babel	Genesis 11:1-9	190 words
Abraham Sacrifices his Only Son Isaac	Genesis 21:1-7, 22:1-14	575 words
The Ladder to Heaven	Genesis 28:10-22	365 words
Joseph and Potiphar's Wife	Genesis 39:1-23	650 words
Joseph Sold as a Slave	Genesis 37:12-36	660 words
Joseph's Dreams	Genesis 37:2-11	280 words
Joseph in Prison	Genesis 40:1-23	570 words
Joseph's Dreams Come True	Genesis 41:1-56	1400 words

Slavery in Egypt	Exodus 1:8-22	360 words
Moses Hidden at Birth	Exodus 2:1-10	260 words
Moses Kills an Egyptian	Exodus 2:11-25	380 words
Moses Sees a Burning Bush	Exodus 3:1-12	380 words
Moses at the Bitter Waters	Exodus 15:22–27	185 words
Moses: Water from the Rock	Exodus 17:1-6	210 words
Samuel's Birth	1 Samuel 1:1-28	780 words
Samuel Hears God Speaking	1 Samuel 3:1-20	530 words
David and Goliath	1 Samuel 17:1-54	1600 words
David and Bathsheba	2 Samuel 11:1-27	800 words
David Listens to Nathan's Story	2 Samuel 12:1-14	331 words
King Solomon's Wisdom	1 Kings 3:16-28	390 words
Elijah: Proclaims a Drought	1 Kings 17:1-24	690 words
Elijah: Let the Fire Fall	1 Kings 18:17-46	980 words
Elijah: Fainting Fits	1 Kings 19:1-21	720 words
Elijah: Chariot of Fire	2 Kings 2:1-18	650 words
Elisha: Miraculous Provision of Oil	2 Kings 4:1-7	220 words
Elisha: A Dead Boy Raised to Life	2 Kings 4:8-37	885 words
Elisha: Syrian Officer Healed of Leprosy	2 Kings 5:1-27	970 words
Esther's Story	Esther ch 1-10	5500 words
Jonah's Story	Jonah ch 1; 2:1,10; ch 3-4	1100 words
Daniel Defies the King's Order	2 Chron 36:15-20; Dan 1	780 words
Daniel Interprets the King's Dream	Daniel 2:1-19; 24-49	1370 words
Daniel: Fiery Furnace	Daniel 3:1-30	980 words
Daniel: Handwriting On the Wall	Daniel 5:1-31	970 words
Daniel in the Lion's Den	Daniel 6:1-26	860 words
God's Provision-- the Birds and Flowers	Matthew 6:25-33	220 words
Feeding the five thousand (Matt.)	Matthew 14:13-21	230 words
Walking on Water	Matthew 14:22-33	255 words
Demonized Daughter Healed	Matthew 15:21-31	250 words
The Transfiguration	Matthew 17:1-9	200 words
Forgiving Others	Matthew 18:21-35	350 words
Story of the Talents	Matthew 25:14-30	420 words
At the Tomb	Matthew 28:1-10	240 words
A Leper Healed	Mark 1:40-45	140 words

Paralytic Healed	Mark 2:1-12	260 words
Who is in God's Family?	Mark 3:31-35	90 words
The Four Soils	Mark 4:1-20	450 words
Asleep in the Storm	Mark 4:35-41	160 words
The Man Who Lived Among the Dead	Mark 5:1-20	450 words
Jairus's Daughter and a Bleeding Woman	Mark 5:22–43	225+265 words
John the Baptist's Death	Mark 6:14-29	390 words
Feeding the Five Thousand (Mark)	Mark 6:32-44	295 words
Deaf and Mute Man Healed	Mark 7:31-37	155 words
Blind Man Healed	Mark 8:22-26	115 words
Rich Young Ruler	Mark 10:17-31	380 words
Blind Bartimeus	Mark 10:46-52	180 words
Jesus at Age Twelve	Luke 2:40-52	243 words
Testing of Jesus	Luke 4:1-15	300 words
Fishers of Men	Luke 5:1-11	270 words
Jesus Calls a Tax Collector	Luke 5:27-32	120 words
Wise and Foolish Builders	Luke 6:46-49	120 words
A Centurion's Servant Healed	Luke 7:1-10	250 words
Widow's Son Raised	Luke 7:11-17	165 words
A Sinful Woman Anoints Jesus	Luke 7:36-50	400 words
Sending of the Seventy	Luke 10:1-12,16-21	410 words
Story of the Good Samaritan	Luke 10:25-37	300 words
Martha and Mary At Home	Luke 10:38-42	110 words
The Rich Fool	Luke 12:13-21	195 words
A Crippled Woman Healed	Luke 13:10-17	210 words
A Lost Sheep and a Lost Coin	Luke 15:1-10	220 words
The Story of the Lost Son	Luke 15:11-32	530 words
The Story of the Rich Man and the Beggar	Luke 16:19-31	305 words
Ten Lepers Healed	Luke 17:12-19	130 words
Story of the Widow and the Unjust Judge	Luke 18:1-5	100 words
The Pharisee and the Tax Collector	Luke 18:9-14	140 words
Zacchaeus's Story	Luke 19:1-10	200 words
Triumphal Entry	Luke 19:28-40	225 words
Peter's Denial	Luke 22:54-62	175 words
Jesus Crucified with Two Criminals	Luke 23:32-43	240 words

Water into Wine	John 2:1-11	245 words
Nicodemus Comes to Jesus Secretly	John 3:1-21	490 words
The Woman at the Well	John 4:3-30, 39-42	685 words
Jesus Heals a Nobleman's Son	John 4:46-54	210 words
Crippled Man Healed at Pool of Bethesda	John 5:1-15	330 words
Forgiveness of an Adulteress	John 8:2-11	245 words
A Man Born Blind Healed	John 9:1-41	915 words
The Resurrection of Lazarus	John 11:1-46	945 words
Jesus Appears to His Disciples	John 20:19-29	255 words
Feed My Sheep	John 21:1-19	555 words
Jesus Ascends	Acts 1:4-5, 8-11	190 words
Pentecost	Acts 2:1-24, 36-47	755 words
A Crippled Man Is Healed	Acts 3:1-20; Acts 4:1-4	418 words
Peter and John on Trial	Acts 4:5-24, 29-31	545 words
The Punishment of Ananias and Sapphira	Acts 4:32-35; 5:1-16	450 words
Trouble in the Church	Acts 6:1-7	206 words
The Evangelist and the Magician	Acts 8:5-25	480 words
Conversion of the Ethiopian Official	Acts 8:26-39	340 words
Paul's Conversion on the Damascus Road	Acts 9:1-30	730 words
Peter: Tabitha Raised from the Dead	Acts 9:36-43	210 words
Peter and Cornelius, First Gentile Convert	Acts 10:1 to 11:1-4,18	1030 words
Peter Set Free from Jail by Angels	Acts 12:1-24	575 words
Paul's First Missionary Journey	Acts 13:1-12	290 words
Paul and Barnabas are Worshipped	Acts 14:8-18	260 words
Paul and Barnabas Split	Acts 15:36 to 16:12	300 words
Paul and Silas in Jail	Acts 16:13-40	660 words
Paul Plants a Church at Corinth	Acts 18:1-18, 21-22	400 words
Paul: Seven Brothers Flee	Acts 19:11-20	220 words
Paul: Eutychus Falls Asleep in Church	Acts 20:7-12	150 words
Paul: Shipwrecked	Acts 27:1-44	875 words
Paul Bitten by a Poisonous Snake	Acts 28:1-10	270 words

Church Challenge Chart

The Church Challenge Chart on the next three pages is a helpful tool for engaging every member of your small group or church in memorizing God's Word in a fun and unifying way. More specifically, this chart is helpful for determining what books of the Bible your church or small group could collectively memorize if every person in your group memorized only one or two verses.

Before you look at the chart, think about how many people are in your group or church (ten people? one hundred people? one thousand people?). Next think about a book of the Bible that your group or church is planning to study this year or next year. Then look at the chart to see how many verses each person in your group would get to memorize in order to collectively memorize that entire book of the Bible.

Number of People Needed When Memorizing:

TESTAMENT	BOOK	# of Chapters	1 Verse Each	2 Verses Each	5 Verses Each	10 Verses Each	20 Verses Each	30 Verses Each	40 Verses Each	50 Verses Each
NEW	2 JOHN	1	13	7	3	1	1	0	0	0
NEW	3 JOHN	1	14	7	3	1	1	0	0	0
OLD	OBADIAH	1	21	11	4	2	1	1	1	0
NEW	PHILEMON	1	25	13	5	3	1	1	1	1
NEW	JUDE	1	25	13	5	3	1	1	1	1
OLD	HAGGAI	2	38	19	8	4	2	1	1	1
NEW	TITUS	3	46	23	9	5	2	2	1	1
OLD	NAHUM	3	47	24	9	5	2	2	1	1
NEW	2 THESSALONIANS	3	47	24	9	5	2	2	1	1
OLD	JONAH	4	48	24	10	5	2	2	1	1
OLD	ZEPHANIAH	3	53	27	11	5	3	2	1	1
OLD	MALACHI	4	55	28	11	6	3	2	1	1
OLD	HABAKKUK	3	56	28	11	6	3	2	1	1
NEW	2 PETER	3	61	31	12	6	3	2	2	1
OLD	JOEL	3	73	37	15	7	4	2	2	1
NEW	2 TIMOTHY	4	83	42	17	8	4	3	2	2
OLD	RUTH	4	85	43	17	9	4	3	2	2
NEW	1 THESSALONIANS	5	89	45	18	9	4	3	2	2
NEW	COLOSSIANS	4	95	48	19	10	5	3	2	2
NEW	PHILIPPIANS	4	104	52	21	10	5	3	3	2
OLD	MICAH	7	105	53	21	11	5	4	3	2
NEW	1 PETER	5	105	53	21	11	5	4	3	2
NEW	1 JOHN	5	105	53	21	11	5	4	3	2
NEW	JAMES	5	108	54	22	11	5	4	3	2
NEW	1 TIMOTHY	6	113	57	23	11	6	4	3	2
OLD	SONG OF SOLOMON	8	117	59	23	12	6	4	3	2
OLD	AMOS	9	146	73	29	15	7	5	4	3

Number of People Needed When Memorizing:

TESTAMENT	BOOK	# of Chapters	1 Verse Each	2 Verses Each	5 Verses Each	10 Verses Each	20 Verses Each	30 Verses Each	40 Verses Each	50 Verses Each
NEW	GALATIANS	6	149	75	30	15	7	5	4	3
OLD	LAMENTATIONS	5	154	77	31	15	8	5	4	3
NEW	EPHESIANS	6	155	78	31	16	8	5	4	3
OLD	ESTHER	10	167	84	33	17	8	6	4	3
OLD	HOSEA	14	197	99	39	20	10	7	5	4
OLD	ZECHARIAH	14	211	106	42	21	11	7	5	4
OLD	ECCLESIASTES	12	222	111	44	22	11	7	6	4
NEW	2 CORINTHIANS	13	257	129	51	26	13	9	6	5
OLD	EZRA	10	280	140	56	28	14	9	7	6
NEW	HEBREWS	13	303	152	61	30	15	10	8	6
OLD	DANIEL	12	357	179	71	36	18	12	9	7
NEW	REVELATION	22	404	202	81	40	20	13	10	8
OLD	NEHEMIAH	13	406	203	81	41	20	14	10	8
NEW	ROMANS	16	433	217	87	43	22	14	11	9
NEW	1 CORINTHIANS	16	437	219	87	44	22	15	11	9
OLD	JUDGES	21	618	309	124	62	31	21	15	12
OLD	JOSHUA	24	658	329	132	66	33	22	16	13
NEW	MARK	16	678	339	136	68	34	23	17	14
OLD	2 SAMUEL	24	695	348	139	70	35	23	17	14
OLD	2 KINGS	25	719	360	144	72	36	24	18	14
OLD	1 SAMUEL	31	810	405	162	81	41	27	20	16
OLD	1 KINS	22	816	408	163	82	41	27	20	16
OLD	2 CHRONICLES	36	822	411	164	82	41	27	21	16
OLD	LEVITICUS	27	859	430	172	86	43	29	21	17
NEW	JOHN	21	879	440	176	88	44	29	22	18
OLD	PROVERS	31	915	458	183	92	46	31	23	18
OLD	1 CHRONICLES	29	942	471	188	94	47	31	24	19

Number of People Needed When Memorizing:

TESTAMENT	BOOK	# of Chapters	1 Verse Each	2 Verses Each	5 Verses Each	10 Verses Each	20 Verses Each	30 Verses Each	40 Verses Each	50 Verses Each
OLD	DEUTERONOMY	34	959	480	192	96	48	32	24	19
NEW	ACTS	28	1007	504	201	101	50	34	25	20
OLD	JOB	42	1070	535	214	107	54	36	27	21
NEW	MATTHEW	28	1071	536	214	107	54	36	27	21
NEW	LUKE	24	1151	576	230	115	58	38	29	23
OLD	EXODUS	40	1213	607	243	121	61	40	30	24
OLD	EZEKIEL	48	1273	637	255	127	64	42	32	25
OLD	NUMBERS	36	1288	644	258	129	64	43	32	26
OLD	ISAIAH	66	1292	646	258	129	65	43	32	26
OLD	JEREMIAH	52	1364	682	273	136	68	45	34	27
OLD	GENESIS	50	1533	767	307	153	77	51	38	31
OLD	PSALMS	150	2461	1231	492	246	123	82	62	49

Number of People Needed When Memorizing:

	# of Chapters	1 Verse Each	2 Verses Each	5 Verses Each	10 Verses Each	20 Verses Each	30 Verses Each	40 Verses Each	50 Verses Each
NEW TESTAMENT	260	7957	3979	1591	796	398	265	199	159
OLD TESTAMENT	929	23145	11573	4629	2315	1157	772	579	463
WHOLE BIBLE	1189	31102	15551	6220	3110	1555	1037	778	622

Battle Resources

A. Marching Orders

B. Plan of Attack

C. Learning Styles Quiz

D. Example Memorization Plan

E. Review Partner Mark-Up Key

F. The Healthy Brain Diet

G. Other Memorization Resources

H. On-the-Go Memorization Tactics for Life's Busy Seasons

I. Active Memorization Ground Rules

Bible Memorization Marching Orders

Aaron's Sample Bible Memorization Marching Orders

Essentials Track
Life Verse: *Philippians 3:8*
Gospel Verses: *Rom. 3:23 & 6:23; Eph. 2:8–9; John 3:16; 1 Cor. 15:1–3*
Temptation/Fear Fighters: *1 Corinthians 6:12–20 (Battling Lust)*

Growing Track
Three-Verse Challenge: *Philippians 3:8–10*
Psalm of Your Age: *Psalm 34*
Favorite Chapter: *Philippians 3*

Sharing Track
Prayer in the Bible: *Daniel 9:3–19 (Personal and Corporate Confession)*
Memorize a Tellable Bible Story: *A Crippled Man Is Healed (Acts 3:1-20)*
Five-Minute Gospel Presentation for the Stage: *The Arsenal 6*

Knowing Track
Prophecy in the Bible: *1 Thessalonians 4:13–18*
Favorite Small Book of the Bible (or multi-chapter passage): *Philippians*
Favorite Large Book of the Bible: *Revelation*

Note: My life verse, three-verse challenge, and favorite chapter are all within my favorite small book of the Bible—Philippians. You may find similar overlap as you build your own Bible Memorization Marching Orders. This is good; it will help you build momentum as you move through each track. Also, you will see that I chose a shorter version of "A Crippled Man is Healed " than the recommended passage length in the 110 Tellable Bible Stories from section 10 of The Arsenal. Feel free to make those types of adjustments as you select your passages.

On the next page create your own Bible Memorization Marching Orders.

My Bible Memorization Marching Orders

Essentials Track

Life Verse: _____

Gospel Verses: _____

Temptation/Fear Fighters: _____

Growing Track

Three-Verse Challenge _____

Psalm of your age:_____

Favorite Chapter:_____

Sharing Track

Prayer in the Bible: _____

Memorize a Tellable Bible Story: _____

Five-Minute Gospel Presentation for the stage:
(section 6 of The Arsenal)

Knowing Track

Prophecy in the Bible: _____

Favorite Small Book of the Bible
(or multi-chapter passage): _____

Favorite Large Book of the Bible: _____

Plan of Attack

Write your chosen passage.

_____

Know Why

What is the reason I am memorizing this passage in the Bible? (For example, it could be related to life verse, gospel verse, temptation fighter, fear fighter, growing in my walk with God, knowing him better, encourage others, to be able to pray this passage, etc.)

_____

_____

_____

Know How

Plan It

1. Secure your accountability partner.

    List two options for an accountability partner in the blanks below. Ask your first option if he or she is ready to serve in this way. If that person declines, ask your second option. Then plan to meet with your accountability partner at a specified place and time on a weekly, biweekly, or monthly basis. Ask your accountability partner to memorize a passage of his or her choice with you. When you meet, ask each other how your Bible memorization is going, listen to each other quote what you've memorized up to that point, share what God is teaching you through that passage, and encourage each other to stay on track.

    a. _____

    b. _____

2.   Calculate how long it will take you to memorize your passage. Or download the Personal Memorization Plan Calculator at www.warriorsofthewordbook.org/resources.

How many verses per day/week do you plan to memorize?

_____

How many days a week will you be memorizing?

_____

When do you plan to start memorizing? _____

Based on how many verses are in your chosen passage and your answers to the previous three questions, when should your deadline for completing the passage be? _____

_____

3.   Determine a good location and time of day for you to accomplish your Bible memorization. List two places you could potentially memorize. Be sure they are locations where you feel alone and have limited distractions: Remember to choose a time of day where you are alert and have a clear mind.

a.   _____

b.   _____

4.   Schedule a time to share your passage with others before you start memorizing. This will give you further accountability and motivation when the going gets tough! Schedule your passage sharing time for two weeks after your memorization deadline to give yourself some time to review and solidify what you have learned so that you can share with confidence. When you share your passage with your small group, be sure to tell them what God has taught you through this passage and how memorizing it has affected your daily walk with him. Based on your anticipated memorization completion date, when would be a good date to schedule a Scripture Sharing Celebration of your passage for your church or a small group of your friends or family?

_____

_____

List two group options in which you could schedule a time to share your passage for your church or a small group of friends. This is best done as a part of a regularly scheduled meeting time. Ask your first option. If that does not work out, ask your second option.

a. _____

b. _____

Understand It

In your own words, what seems to be the main point of this passage?

_____

_____

Paraphrase the passage in your own words:

_____

_____

_____

_____

Look at your study Bible notes, a Bible commentary, or search the internet to find the answers to the following:

Who wrote this passage? _____

Who did they write it to? _____

When did they write it? _____

Where was the writer when writing? _____

Where was the receiver of the message when it was written?

_____

Why was this passage written?_____

_____

_____

See It, Say It, Do It

List at least four memorization techniques you will try during your Active Memorization process. Feel free to reference the Active Memorization Ground Rules and Tactics to Try in section I of Battle Resources.

1._____

2._____

3._____

4._____

Review It

List two places and times of the day where you could potentially review. (Remember that review can be done while multitasking!):

1._____

2._____

Apply It

How can I apply this passage right now? _____

_____

_____

_____

Repeat

What passage(s) are you going to memorize next?

_____

_____

Learning Styles Quiz

Circle the answer that best applies to you:

1. I want to assemble a plastic model airplane that came in parts. I would learn best from

   a. written instructions and diagrams showing each stage of the assembly.
   b. advice from someone who has done it before.
   c. watching a video of a person assembling the model airplane.

2. I want to learn how to take better photos. The first thing I would do is

   a. read the camera's instructions and printed diagrams of its features.
   b. ask questions of an experienced photographer friend and talk about the camera and its features.
   c. start taking pictures using various techniques and with different settings and compare the resulting photos.

3. I want to learn about a new project that has been assigned to me. I would ask for

   a. a written description of the project with requirements and main objectives.
   b. an opportunity to discuss the project.
   c. examples of previous similar projects.

4. I have finished a competition or test and I would like some feedback. I would prefer feedback that

   a. uses a written description of my results with visual markings.

   b. is from somebody who talks it through with me.
   c. uses examples from what I have done rather than examples of how I could do better.

5. I want to learn to do something new on a computer. I would

   a. read the written instructions that came with the program.
   b. talk with people who know about the program.
   c. start using it and learn by trial and error.

6. I prefer a presenter or teacher who uses

    a. handouts, books, diagrams, charts, graphs, maps, or readings.
    b. question and answer, talk, group discussion, or guest speakers.
    c. demonstrations, models, or practical application sessions.

7. When I give someone directions to my house, I am most likely to relay to them

    a. a description of buildings and landmarks they will pass along the way.
    b. the names of the roads or streets they will be on.
    c. "Follow me; it will be easier if I just show you how to get there."

8. When in a new place, I find my way around by

    a. looking for a map or a directory that shows me where everything is.
    b. asking someone for directions.
    c. exploring until I find what I'm looking for.

9. The best way for me to learn how something (like a computer or a video game) works is

    a. reading about it.
    b. getting someone else to demonstrate it for me.
    c. figuring it out on my own.

10. When learning my multiplication tables, I learned best by

    a. writing them over and over.
    b. repeating them out loud while reviewing flashcards.
    c. creating a game out of practicing with a parent or friend.

11. I have a problem with my tooth and have to have a procedure. I would prefer the dentist to:

    a. give me something to read to explain the problem and the ensuing procedure.
    b. describe what is wrong and the details of the procedure.
    c. show me a plastic model in order to explain the problem and procedure.

12. I want to play a new board game with friends. I would prefer to

    a. study the instructions myself.
    b. have the rules explained to me verbally.
    c. jump in to play the game, learning as we play.

13. When learning a dance, I would learn best by
    a. watching someone else do the dance moves first.
    b. having the steps verbally explained to me.
    c. jumping in and attempting to do it with the instructor.

14. When learning a sport, a new skill will stick best when I
    a. watch someone else do it.
    b. am given a verbal explanation of how to do it.
    c. try different self-discovered moves and techniques until I figure out what works best.

Short Answer Questions

• What was your favorite subject in school when you were growing up?

_____

• Why did you like it? _____

_____

• What subject was your least favorite and why did you dislike it?

_____

_____

• Can you make any discoveries about how your teacher taught, how the information was presented, why you remembered some pieces of information but not others, or why you liked or disliked the class or subject?

_____

_____

_____

Tally your responses from the multiple choice questions above:

How many A answers did you have?_____

How many B answers did you have? _____

How many C answers did you have? _____

A = Visual
B = Auditory
C = Kinesthetic

Compare your tallied multiple choice results with your answers to the short-answer questions. Do they confirm each other? What did you discover is your top learning style? What learning styles come in second and third place for you? Write them in the blanks below in order of effectiveness for your own learning.

My Learning Styles Order

1._____

2,_____

3,_____

Example Memorization Plan

The example memorization plan on the next page gives you an idea of how the different phases of memorization should be incorporated into your personal memorization experience. Breaking down the task of memorizing a passage of Scripture into these attainable steps and phases will be both encouraging and empowering as you seek to successfully hide God's Word in your heart.

Personal Memorization Plan Calculator

We have created a Bible memorization planning tool just for you! Just go to www.warriorsofthewordbook.org/resources. Here you can download the Personal Memorization Plan Calculator, which is an excel program that will create a custom Bible memorization plan based on the length of your chosen passage and the number of verses you plan to memorize each day. The program even builds in your review and catch up days for you. This is the fastest and easiest way to create a detailed plan for your next Bible memorization project. We know you will be blessed by this simple and helpful tool. Download it today for free!

Example Memorization Plan

For memorizing one chapter (thirty verses) at a rate of one verse per day

	Pre-Memorization	
DAY 1	✔ Read the entire chapter ✔ Read the chapters before and after it ✔ Read some background on the who, what, when, where, why, and how of this passage	
DAY 2	✔ Read the chosen chapter once ✔ Look up any unfamiliar words ✔ Read any commentary on the passage as needed ✔ Paraphrase the chapter in your own words	

	ACTIVE MEMORIZATION	SOLIDIFICATION REVIEW	MAINTENANCE REVIEW
DAY 3	Verse 1		
DAY 4	Verse 2	Verse 1	
DAY 5	Verse 3	Verses 1-2	
DAY 6	Verse 4	Verses 1-3	
DAY 7	Verse 5	Verses 1-4	
DAY 8	Verse 6	Verses 1-5	
DAY 9	Verse 7	Verses 1-6	
DAY 10	Verse 8	Verses 1-7	
DAY 11	Verse 9	Verses 2-8	
DAY 12	Verse 10	Verses 3-9	
DAY 13	Verse 11	Verses 4-10	
DAY 14	Verse 12	Verses 5-11	
DAY 15	Verse 13	Verses 6-12	
DAY 16	Verse 14	Verses 7-13	Verses 1-6
DAY 17	Verse 15	Verses 8-14	
DAY 18	Verse 16	Verses 9-15	
DAY 19	Verse 17	Verses 10-16	
DAY 20	Verse 18	Verses 11-17	
DAY 21	Verse 19	Verses 12-18	
DAY 22	Verse 20	Verses 13-19	
DAY 23	Verse 21	Verses 14-20	Verses 1-13
DAY 24	Verse 22	Verses 15-21	
DAY 25	Verse 23	Verses 16-22	
DAY 26	Verse 24	Verses 17-23	
DAY 27	Verse 25	Verses 18-24	
DAY 28	Verse 26	Verses 19-25	
DAY 29	Verse 27	Verses 20-26	
DAY 30	Verse 28	Verses 21-27	Verses 1-20
DAY 31	Verse 29	Verses 22-28	
DAY 32	Verse 30	Verses 23-29	
DAY 33		Verses 24-30	Verses 1-30
DAY 34		Verses 25-30	Verses 1-30
DAY 35		Verses 26-30	Verses 1-30
DAY 36		Verses 27-30	Verses 1-30
DAY 37		Verses 28-30	Verses 1-30

Review Partner Mark-Up Key

The Review Partner Mark-Up Key on the next page is a tool to help you be a good review partner. It will show you how to mark up a Bible passage in a way that is helpful for your friend to correct any mistakes made in reciting it.

Making these kinds of markings for your friend is much more effective than the ever-so-tempting approach of interrupting him or her every few seconds to give a verbal critique. When your friend finishes reciting the passage, encourage him or her for all the hard work, and give the Bible or paper with your markings to facilitate memorization corrections.

Feel free to clarify what your markings mean if you feel they are unclear. Also, feel free to make up your own markings if your brain works differently than ours.

Please note: You should only speak during the recitation if your friend who is quoting asks you to give him or her the next word or phrase. This should be done by the quoter simply saying "line." Once "line" is called, the review partner gives the next word or short phrase to the person quoting. You should give as little as you think the quoter needs to keep going. This is not an exact science but is rather something that is learned through trial and error as you work together as a team.

Paraphrased 〰️

Example:　We　are　ambassadors　for　Christ

Omitted ⬭

Example:　We　are　ambassadors （for　Christ）

Inserted Word/Phrase ^

Jesus
ᵛ
Example:　We　are　ambassadors　for　Christ

Swapped Words/Phrases ↶↷

Example:　We　are　ambassadors　for　Christ

Paused *

Example:　We　are*ambassadors　for　Christ

Prompted /

Example:　We　are　ambassadors/for　Christ

Needs Work ▭

Example:　We　are　ambassadors　for　Christ

A Healthy Brain Diet

Emerging research indicates that the ketones in medium-chain triglycerides feed the brain and help it function optimally. An easy way to consume these is through unrefined coconut oil or MCT oil. Some other supplements that may help with memory retention and alertness are vitamin B12, choline (from lecithin), Dr. Schultze's Brain Formula, and increased circulation. See *Be Your Own Doctor* by Rachel Weaver, Share-A-Care Publications, 2010.

If you would like to do more research, consider reading *Alzheimer's Disease: What If There Was a Cure?* Second Edition by Dr. Mary T. Newport, 2013.

Other Bible Memorization Resources

Scripture Memory Fellowship. *SwordGrip*. Scripture Memory. scripturememory.com/catalog/category/view/s/swordgrip/id/47/. (SwordGrip is a challenge to memorize one set of three consecutive verses from every book of the Bible, and the resources to do it with ease.)

Scripture Memory Fellowship. *VerseLocker App* . scripturememory. com. Scripturememory.com/mobile.

Truth78. *Fighter Verses App*. Fighterverses.com/resources/.

Millennial Apps, LLC. *The Bible Memory App*. biblememory.com.

Dwell. Dwell Bible Memory Temporary Tattoos. Dwell Differently. dwelldifferently.com.

The Navigators. *Topical Memory System* and *Topical Memory System: Life Issues*. navigators.org/resource/topical-memory-system. (see pages 55 and 196)

Dorothy A. Miller *Simply the Story Handbook*. The God's Story Project. Hemet, CA, 2006, 2011. Simplythestory.org/downloads/handbook/handbookSTSDraft03-23-11.pdf . PDF. (A 160-page free resource in multiple languages; see page 61 and 166)

Laughlin, Marquis. *How to Memorize Anything: The Fast, Fun And Easy Way!* Marquis Laughlin Ministries, digital download. https://actsoftheword.com/product/how-to-memorize-anything-the-fast-fun-and-easy-way/.

Other Recommendations

Platt, David. *Radical: Taking Back Your Faith from the American Dream*. Colorado Springs, Colorado: Multnomah Books, 2010. (see page 11)

Koehler, Paul. *Telling God's Stories with Power: Biblical Storytelling in Oral Cultures.* William Carey Library, 2010.
(see page 199)

Evangelism Explosion. "Share Your Faith Workshop."
Evangelismexplosion.org/ministries/share-your-faith/.

Boa, Kenneth. *Face to Face: Praying the Scriptures for Intimate Worship.* Grand Rapids, Michigan: Zondervan Publishing House, 1997. (see page 61)

Foer, Joshua. *Moonwalking with Einstein: The Art and Science of Remembering.* New York: Penguin Group , 2011.
(see pages 35, 38-39, 121 and 138)

Lorayne, Harry and Jerry Lucas. *The Memory Book: The Classic Guide to Improving Your Memory at Work, School, and at Play.* New York: Ballantine Books, an imprint of The Random House Publishing Group. 1974.

Cloud, Henry. *The Power of the Other: The Startling Effect Other People Have on You, from the Boardroom to the Bedroom and Beyond—and What to Do About It.* New York: HarperCollins Publishers. 2016.
(see page 93)

Strong, James. *Strong's Exhaustive Concordance of the Bible.* Peabody, Massachusetts: Hendrickson Publishing. 2009 (also available from other publishers).
(see page 102)

Newport, Mary T. *Alzheimer's Disease: What If There Was a Cure?* Second edition. Laguna Beach, CA: Basic Health Publications. 2013.
(see page 225)

Bible Gateway. biblegateway.com
(see pages 56 and 148)

Goerke, Matthew. "The Memory Switch." MemorySwitch.com.
(see page 34)

BATTLE RESOURCES: H

On-the-Go Memorization Tactics for Life's Busy Seasons

Whether you are an overwhelmed parent, a busy professional, a harried pastor, a preoccupied teenager, or a senior citizen, you can do some practical things to memorize God's Word in pockets of time throughout your day. These creative ideas will enable you to memorize God's Word even while you are on the go.

1. **Make some pocket-sized Scripture memory cards you can keep with you while you are on the go.** Anytime you have a free minute (waiting for your food in the microwave, waiting for class to start, sitting at a doctor's office, and so on) pull out your cards and memorize or review. These "margin minutes" are where we usually pull out our phones and check Facebook, texts, or emails. How much better to use those minutes to memorize the Word of God!

2. **Write Bible verses on note cards or pieces of note paper and post them anywhere and everywhere you frequent.** We have a friend who taped her memory verses to her water bottle, so whenever she was trying to memorize or quote, she could just look down quickly and continue to work on it.

3. **Keep a Bible (or tape some Bible verse cards) in the bathroom**. Every time you use the bathroom, instead of being on your phone or reading a book, you can review your verses.

4. **Use a Bible Memory App on your phone** like VerseLocker by Scripture Memory Fellowship or Fighter Verses. These clever applications can help you memorize using many of the techniques talked about in chapter 6 of this book. One downside to using an app on your phone is the potential of getting distracted by texts, social media notifications, or phone

calls. It is ideal to do Scripture memorization away from such distractions. So be warned that, if you use a smartphone application, you may want to put your phone on Do Not Disturb or turn off your data while you memorize.

5. **Listen to your chosen passage using an audio Bible while you drive or do housework**. You would be surprised how easy it is to memorize a passage after listening to it twice a day for two weeks. After listening to the passage every day for a couple of weeks, set aside several ten-to-fifteen-minute segments of time to do some Active Memorization, then go back to listening to your audio Bible each day. You will now be able to review by quoting along with the audio Bible. One game that is fun to play is trying to quote the verses faster than the audio Bible, beating it to each word!

6. **Voice record verses or passages on your phone and listen to them every day when you drive** in the car or while doing housework. Although this takes one more step than simply using an audio Bible, this can be even more effective. When you hear the words in your own voice and your own inflection, it can help the words and meaning soak in deeper.

Active Memorization Ground Rules

- Use all three learning styles
- Memorize phrase by phrase
- Never memorize silently
- Pray before you begin
- Sit up straight or stand
- Memorize the thoughts, not just the words
- Experience it
- Have fun

Active Memorization Tactics to Try

SEE IT	SAY IT	DO IT
Write it	Sing it	Use hand motions
Draw it	Record it	Dance it
Game it	Vary inflection/intention	Act it
Acronyms	Use accents/voices	Type it

Be a good teacher to yourself

Use All Three Learning Styles!

Acknowledgements

Emily and I would like to thank everyone that contributed to the creation of this book.

First, I must thank my beautiful wife and co-author, Emily. I never would have been able to do this without you. Your incredible writing skills have made this book extremely relatable and easy to read. Congrats on fulfilling a lifelong dream of publishing your first book. I love you more than I can say.

To my mom and dad, Peggy and Glenn House, thank you for being amazing godly influences in my life, for guiding me through every season growing up, and for hosting grandparent camp for our kids more than once so that we could write and edit this book.

To my brother, Cliff House, thank you for always being there for me through every struggle and for your wisdom and accountability.

To my sister, Amber House, thank you for being my biggest fan, and for courageously memorizing God's Word even though it is difficult for you.

To Esther Eaton, thank you for starting this project with us back in 2017 as a Piercing Word intern and for being the editor of our first manuscript draft that we did in 2019. Also, thanks for being such a huge encouragement and cheerleader along the way.

To Diane Omondi, thank you for your edits and encouragements.

To Kelli Sallman, thank you for your incredible insight into the overall structure of the book and helping us to tell our story well.

To Linda Harris, thank you for your thorough copy edits, your encouragements, and for your insights as one who has different learning style strengths than us.

To Sarah Sauder, thank you for shepherding us along the book publication process and for beautifully formatting this book.

To Caleb Hughes, thank you for driving the creativity and detail for the book cover design and images throughout the book. Thank you also for helping us streamline the theme of this book throughout. Your creativity and encouragement along the way has been a huge blessing!

AARON

To Katie Moser, thank you for proofreading and working through manuscript formatting issues. We are so thankful for your kind heart and your detail-oriented brain!

To Dan Lehning, thank you for creating the Five Verse Gospel chart, the Example Memorization Plan chart, and Church Challenge chart. You are a wizard with Excel!

To Stephen Cahill, thank you for creating such beautiful graphic designs for the book cover and interior of the book.

To Hannah Orneles, thank you for creating the Scripture artwork examples in this book.

To Roy Russell, thank you for helping to finance the publishing of this book and providing motivation, advice, and encouragement along the way as a friend and Piercing Word Board Member.

To Mark and Helene Hoffman, thank you for helping to finance the publishing of this book and for your advice and encouragement along the way as friends and Piercing Word Board Members.

To our other current Piercing Word Board Members- Nathanael Waite, Michael Lapham, Nevin and Glori Brubaker, and my parents, thank you for your tireless support, encouragement, and advice.

To Keith and Anna Zimmerman, thank you for helping to finance the publishing of this book. Also, thank you Darlene Herod, Octavia Boutte, and Lindsay Van Sicklen for your financial support.

To JT Schaeffer, thank you for suggesting that Emily and I take a week away to write this book. I don't think this book would be here without that God-inspired suggestion.

To Deryl Hurst, thank you for inspiring the title of this book. *Warriors of the Word* has stuck ever since you called our Bible Memorization term group at Dove Westgate Church by that name several years ago!

To Rhonda Bedee and Chris Nissley, thank you for proofreading this book in record time before printing.

To David Platt, thank you for being the spark that inspired my very first Scripture Performance.

To Lee Emerson, thank you for teaching me how to memorize and love God's Word deeply in Bible Drill when I was a teenager.

To my mom and dad, Steve and Cheryl Douglass, thank you for raising me to have a deep love for scripture and for your personal example of clinging to God's Word. Thank you both for your constant encouragement, prayers, and support for Aaron and me, and for watching our kids more times than we can count! Dad, you have always been my biggest fan when it came to my writing - thank you for always believing in me and pushing me to give wings to my dreams.

To our darling children, Caleb, Aria Joy, and Malakai: thank you for enthusiastically hiding God's Word in your heart and for joyously allowing grandparents and babysitters take over for a while so mom and dad could steal away to write this book. You are the best kids in the whole world!

To my Aaron, my love, my teammate: I am so proud of you for sharing your story, your journey, your God-given insights with the world. I am proud of you for saying "yes" to this big crazy adventure of Scripture memory, Scripture performance, and full-time ministry. Thank you for choosing me to dance this journey with you. I love doing *everything* with you - whether it is raising babies, sharing the Gospel, washing dishes, or writing a book - we truly are better together.

To our babysitters, Abby Weiss, Doreen Scott, Sarah Joy Fogle, Ellie Hollinger, Julia Hollinger, and Lexi Fisher, thank you for enabling us to complete this book and for taking such amazing care of our kids.

To Biff and Rhonda Adam, thank you for letting us use your cabin to write the original draft of this book. It was a blessing to have such a quiet, beautiful, and inspiring atmosphere where we could think and write.

Also, a huge thank you to everyone who shared with us Victory Stories to be implemented into this book. Your stories are encouraging many others who seek to know God better through his Word.

More than anything, we give praise to God our Father and the Lord Jesus Christ. This is his book. He has carried us through every struggle and to every victory and continues to lead and guide us every step of the way. To him be all the glory both now and forever! Amen.

EMILY

Endnotes

Chapter 2

[1] Joshua Foer, *Moonwalking with Einstein: The Art and Science of Remembering Everything* (New York, Penguin Group. 2011), 13.

[2] James Gilchrist Lawson, ed., *Cyclopedia of Religious Anecdotes*, (New York; Chicago: Fleming H. Revell Co., 1923), 303.

Chapter 3

[3] Kendall F. Haven, *Story Proof: The Science Behind the Startling Power of Story* (Westport, CT, Libraries Unlimited, 2007), 16–17.

Chapter 4

[4] Henry Cloud, *The Power of the Other* (New York, HarperCollins Publishers, 2016).

[5] "Accountability." Google's English Dictionary, Oxford University Press 2020.

Chapter 8

[6] Foer, *Moonwalking with Einstein*, 269–270.

Chapter 9

[7] *Simply The Story Handbook*. (A 160-page, free resource in multiple languages)

http://simplythestory.org/oralbiblestories/index.php?option=com_content&view=article&id=52&Itemid=228#education

About the Authors

Aaron House is the Founder and Executive Director of **Piercing Word.** Although originally from Houston, Texas, he currently lives in Lancaster, Pennsylvania, with his lovely wife, Emily House, and their three children. Before Piercing Word ministry became full time, he was a full-time professional actor at Sight & Sound Theatres in Lancaster, Pennsylvania, for three years as well as the Branson, Missouri, location for two years. He has a BA in Musical Theatre from Ouachita Baptist University in Arkansas and has been performing professionally since he was ten years old. After moving to Lancaster, Aaron met Emily through mutual friends at a swing dancing event and got to know her by joining her Bible study small group. They married in October 2012. Just a few months later, God gave both of them the faith to take the ministry full time in January 2013. Aaron was ordained as a minister of the gospel at Champion Forest Baptist Church in Houston, Texas, in November 2013. He has a fiery zeal for Jesus Christ and for the Word of God. He desires to enable other believers to truly know God through his Word and wield the sword of the Spirit in their everyday lives.

Emily House has been involved with **Piercing Word** since 2011. She attended Elim Bible Institute. She was an Assistant Director of DRAMA Ministry in Lancaster, Pennsylvania. Emily has been an avid writer since childhood and is thrilled to publish her first book with her husband. God has given her a fervent passion to disciple other believers. She is honored to have the opportunity to help equip fellow believers in the memorization of God's precious Word. Emily loves working alongside her husband in the ministry as well as in their home, where they disciple their three beautiful, rambunctious children: Caleb, Aria Joy, and Malakai. The family lives in Akron, Pennsylvania, and are members of Dove Westgate Church in Ephrata.

The History of Piercing Word

"Keep doing this until I tell you to stop"

When I was a junior in college, I stepped into a chapel service led by David Platt, author of the book *Radical*—a book I highly recommend. He opened the service by saying, "Please open your Bibles to Romans chapter one." He began to read. About halfway through the chapter, I looked up and realized that he wasn't reading. He was quoting! *He's going to quote the first chapter of Romans!* I thought.

And he did. Then he quoted chapter two . . . chapter three . . . chapter four. Eight chapters later he stopped and gave us a challenge to memorize the Word of God. Fifteen hundred students, including myself, came away from that chapel service profoundly stirred and inspired.

During college, I had started a drama team at a local church. After Platt's challenge, I told one of my fellow college drama team members, "If he as a pastor can rattle off eight chapters of the book of Romans with very little emotion or expression, and we can come away from that so impacted, how much more so can we as actors memorize and internalize the Word of God and present it in a way that is even more impactful?"

The two of us decided to memorize the book of James together. When we performed it for our local church, God's Spirit moved more powerfully than in any other drama we had ever done or seen up to that point. The response from the congregation afterward was overwhelmingly positive and brimming with emotional and spiritual intensity. So we said, "Let's do this again!" We got the whole team together, five actors at that time, and memorized the book of Ephesians. Once again, God's Spirit moved mightily.

A few days later, as I was about to walk into another college chapel service, a woman came up to me crying. Through tears, she thanked me for sharing the Word of God from the stage in such a potent way. She shared how much God had used it in her life. I was overwhelmed with God's Spirit as I left that conversation and entered a time of worship in the chapel. I knelt before the Lord and wept, feeling so unworthy to be used by the Lord in this way. As I worshiped, God

AARON

impressed on my heart that I needed to continue doing this until he told me to stop. That was 2006. In 2007, we incorporated under the name of Piercing Word in Houston. We continued to do dramatic performances with scripts using only the biblical text. Piercing Word went with me around the country as a part-time ministry for the next five years as I performed as a full-time actor in several states. By 2012, Piercing Word had grown to doing twenty-three Scripture Performances over the course of the year.

In 2013, I quit my full time job as an actor by faith, and Emily and I took the ministry full-time. At the same time, I committed to memorizing the New Testament in one year. I did this to inspire others to memorize the Word of God for themselves, to raise funds, and to demonstrate my commitment to the ministry. Over the next few years, Piercing Word grew in its ability to accomplish its mission. In 2019 alone, over sixty Piercing Word team members presented the Word of God in over 250 Scripture Performances. God has continued to have his hand upon this ministry ever since.

PIERCING WORD

piercingword.org

WHO WE ARE

Piercing Word is a group of theatre professionals who love coming alongside Christian leaders to engage people with the Word of God through live Scripture Performances. We exist to *ignite passion for the Word of God in the heart of the Church.* We challenge everyone, everywhere we go to memorize and study God's Word for themselves and equip them to do so by providing discipleship resources including our Bible Memorization Workshops.

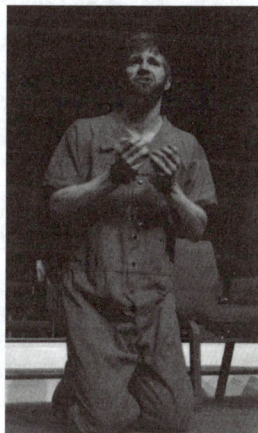

WHERE DO WE GO?

We are based in Lancaster, Pennsylvania and perform for churches, conferences, ministry outreaches, special events and more! Most performances are within a two-hour radius of Lancaster, with occasional regional tours of the United States.

HOW CAN YOU SEE US?

1) **Bring us to your church or event**

Call (888) 244-3461 or visit our website at piercingword.org and click "Request a Booking."

2) **Visit us at one of our scheduled performances**

You can see our full schedule of Scripture Performances at: piercingword.org/events.

3) **Download our Scripture Performance Resources**

Visit piercingword.org/resources to enjoy our digital library of SCRIPTUREvideos, SCRIPTUREscripts, SCRIPTUREmusic, and more!

THE PIERCING WORD PROMISE

BIBLICALLY SOUND & ARTISTICALLY EXCELLENT

Every performance is word-for-word from the ESV Bible, created by a team of theatre professionals in order to highlight the truths of God's Word in creative and powerful ways.

STRESS-FREE PLANNING & EXECUTION

We will help you select a Scripture Performance from our season that will compliment your current study and age group. We will send you all the marketing materials you need for your event and bring a fully equipped team with our own props, costumes, and audio equipment.

AFFORDABLE PARTNERSHIPS

We work with every group to find affordable ways to help cover the costs of our Scripture Performances and Bible Memorization Workshops.

MORE OPPORTUNITIES

Piercing Word offers many additional opportunities beyond our live performances including international tours to Israel and Greece, summer camps and more! For more information on all that Piercing Word has to offer, please visit piercingword.org.

SUPPORT THE MISSION

MAKE A TAX-DEDUCTIBLE DONATION - If you were blessed by the contents of this book, please consider making a donation to support the ministry. Piercing Word is a 501(c)3, non-profit ministry and all donations are tax-deductible. Thank you for partnering with us in this way! Give at piercingword.org/donate.

SIGN UP FOR OUR EMAIL NEWSLETTER - Sign up for our monthly email newsletter where you can stay informed with the latest news and updates. Sign up at piercingword.org/email.

Piercingword.org

PIERCING WORD

Follow us on social media: